Crowdsourcing of Sensor Cloud Services

Azadeh Ghari Neiat • Athman Bouguettaya

Crowdsourcing of Sensor Cloud Services

 Springer

Azadeh Ghari Neiat
School of Information Technologies
University of School of
Information Technologies
NSW, Australia

Athman Bouguettaya
School of Information Technologies
University of Sydney
NSW, Australia

ISBN 978-3-030-08269-7   ISBN 978-3-319-91536-4   (eBook)
https://doi.org/10.1007/978-3-319-91536-4

Printed on acid-free paper

This Springer imprint is published by the registered company Springer International Publishing AG part
of Springer Nature.
The registered company address is: Gewerbestrasse 11, 6330 Cham, Switzerland

To my parents, Aliakbar and Fereshteh, my brothers, Armin and Arash, and my sisters, Parisa and Zari.

Azadeh Ghari Neiat

To my wife and best companion and friend, Malika.

Athman Bouguettaya

Foreword

Recent technological advances allow everyday physical objects to be connected to the Internet and provide their services on the Web. The Internet of Things (IoT), which is widely regarded as the leading technology that will change our world in the coming decade, offers the capability to integrate and connect both digital and physical entities. With a network of cheap sensors and interconnected things, the information we collect about our world will be generated at a much higher granularity from IoT devices. Successful deployment of IoT solutions will allow for safer roads, better use of public transport and cities, effective and cheaper aged care and healthcare, better use of our energy resources, to name a few.

The large amount of real-time sensor data streaming from IoT is a challenging issue because of storage capacity, processing power, and data management constraints. Cloud computing is a promising technology to support the scalable storage and processing of the ever-increasing amount of data. There are a variety of books on the market that cover interesting issues related to IoT. However, to my knowledge, only this book provides a comprehensive overview of the transformation of IoT into services. This book takes a unique approach to integrating sensor-based things (IoT sensors), cloud computing, and service-oriented computing. Such sensor cloud services provide unique capabilities and opportunities for efficient and real-time delivery of IoT services to end users. This book is the first attempt of its kind to provide a holistic view of the issues related to the services in a sensor cloud environment by taking into account the spatio-temporal related challenges. The book provides a detailed treatise of spatio-temporal selection and composition of sensor cloud services. One interesting part of this book is the exploration of crowdsourcing as the vehicle to sense data. The specific and important issues related to crowdsourcing of services in sensor cloud environments are addressed. The book overviews key findings from the authors' experience in analyzing a large number of real-world sensor cloud services. The extensive references included in this book will help the interested readers find out more information on the discussed topics.

It is a real pleasure to have been asked to provide the foreword for this book. I am happy to commend the authors for their outstanding accomplishment, and to inform the readers that they are looking at a true state of the art in the vibrant and rapidly expanding field of IoT services.

Macquarie University   Michael Sheng
Sydney, NSW, Australia
February 2018

Preface

The ubiquity of mobile devices has elicited the emergence of the important domain of crowdsourced sensor cloud services. In this framework, the cloud provides the ideal solution for storing, processing, and managing continuous streams of crowdsourced sensed data. We propose to harness the service paradigms, a key mechanism to transform crowdsourced raw data into useful service-ready information. In our framework, sensors are fixed or crowdsourced and provide streaming sensor data which is stored and managed in the cloud. Services are the abstraction through which this data is transformed to suit users' needs (functional) and requirements/expectations (non-functional, also called Quality of Service (QoS)). The combination of functional and non-functional aspects provide the abstraction of a service that represents crowdsourced sensor cloud services.

In this book, we design and develop a crowdsourced sensor cloud framework with special emphasis on spatio-temporal service selection and composition. We propose a new, two-level composition model for crowdsourced sensor cloud services based on dynamic features including spatio-temporal aspects. The proposed approach is based on a formal sensor cloud service model that abstracts the functional and non-functional aspects of sensor data in the cloud in terms of spatio-temporal features. A spatio-temporal indexing technique is proposed that is based on the 3D R-tree, enabling fast identification of appropriate sensor cloud services. Our novel quality model considers dynamic features of sensors to select and compose sensor cloud services. This model introduces a new QoS as a service which is formulated as a composition of crowdsourced sensor cloud services. We present new QoS-aware spatio-temporal composition algorithms to select the optimal composition plan. We present a heuristic failure-proof service composition algorithm for real-time reaction to sensor cloud services which become unavailable because they are no longer spatially or temporally available. We also provide a greedy redistribution algorithm that offers incentives to crowdsourced service providers to achieve optimal balanced crowdsourced coverage within an area.

We have evaluated the performance and effectiveness of the proposed framework. The experimental results show that the proposed composition framework and incentive-based approach have a satisfying scalability as the number of services becomes larger.

NSW, Australia   Azadeh Ghari Neiat
NSW, Australia   Athman Bouguettaya

Acknowledgments

I would like to express my sincerest love, thanks, and deep appreciation to my family for their unconditional love and support. They have been always there for me whenever I needed them. I also owe special thanks to my lovely friend, Mohsen Laali, who made all of this book possible.

Azadeh Ghari Neiat

I would like to thank my family for their unwavering support during my work on this book.

Athman Bouguettaya

The authors of this book would like to extend their sincere gratitude and appreciation to their collaborators for the contribution to this book; in particular, we would like to acknowledge Prof. Timos Sellis and other collaborators in the Sensor Cloud Services Laboratory (SCSLab) at the University of Sydney. Thank you all!

NSW, Australia	Azadeh Ghari Neiat
NSW, Australia	Athman Bouguettaya

Contents

List of Figures

List of Tables

Chapter 1
Introduction

Sensor cloud services provide a framework where sensors, clouds and services need to deliver useful information from a vast amount of sensor data. The premise is that sensors are the vehicle to collect that data. The cloud is the medium of sensor data storage. The service is the paradigm that allows the transformation of data into useful information. In this chapter, we first discuss the motivation behind this research. We then explain the research challenges. Thirdly, we highlight the research objectives. Finally, we discuss the contributions of this book and finish the chapter by introducing the subsequent chapters.

1.1 Motivation

Wireless Sensor Networks (WSNs) consist of a set of spatially distributed autonomous tiny sensing devices, called sensor nodes, to monitor the locality and fetch sensor data about the surroundings [9, 159]. Each sensor node is equipped with one or more sensors, storage, a microprocessor, a transceiver and, in some cases, an actuator. The sensors are capable of sensing physical or environmental phenomena including thermal, optic, acoustic, seismic and acceleration events. On-board microprocessors can program sensor nodes to accomplish complex tasks such as analysing raw data rather than transmitting only what they observe. The transceiver provides wireless connectivity to communicate the observed phenomena of interest [6, 159]. WSNs are being developed to serve a variety of purposes, e.g., health, energy crisis, safety issues, smart cities and life comfort [99].

Storing, processing and managing continuous streams of sensed data pose key challenges, particularly when WSNs are used for large-scale applications. Because of availability, low-cost and fast access to cloud services, the integration of sensors with the cloud (i.e., sensor cloud) provides a unique opportunity to address challenges related to using sensed data [123]. The sensor cloud is a potential

© Springer International Publishing AG, part of Springer Nature 2018
A. Ghari Neiat, A. Bouguettaya, *Crowdsourcing of Sensor Cloud Services*,
https://doi.org/10.1007/978-3-319-91536-4_1

key enabler for storing and accessing large-scale data. A sensor cloud is formally defined by MicroStrains[1] as "a platform for sensor data storage, remote management and visualization that leverages powerful cloud computing technologies to provide data scalability, user programmable analysis and rapid visualization" [9, 109]. The virtualization technique also enables dynamic resource management, which, in turn, increases resource utilization. According to IntelliSys,[2] a sensor cloud is "an infrastructure that allows truly pervasive computation using sensors as an interface between physical and cyber worlds, the data-computed clusters as the cyber backbone and the internet as the communication medium" [9].

A key challenge in the sensor cloud is the efficient and real-time delivery of refined sensor data to end-users. We propose to harness the power and simplicity of the service paradigm with its functional and non-functional components as a key mechanism to turn sensor data into useful information. The service paradigm is a powerful abstraction that hides data-specific information which focuses on *how* data is to be used. In the case of sensor data shared in the cloud, the *functionality* and *non-functional* aspects are abstracted as sensor cloud services. As a result, they become easily accessible irrespective of the distribution of sensor data sources. We propose a *service-oriented sensor cloud architecture* that provides an integrated abstract view of the sensor data shared on the cloud and delivered as sensor cloud services.

The ubiquity of mobile devices such as smartphones has also elicited the emergence of the important domain of crowdsourced sensor data. Mobility is an intrinsic part of the functional and non-functional aspects of sensor cloud services because of the nature of sensors such as smartphones. Therefore, the *position* and *time* of sensed data are of paramount importance, reflecting the spatio-temporal characteristics. In this regard, we focus on spatio-temporal aspects as key parameters to query the sensor cloud.

1.2 Challenges in Spatio-Temporal Composition of Crowdsourced Sensor Cloud Services

In the setting of the sensor cloud, existing service selection and composition approaches mostly assume a static data environment. We identify the following research challenges.

- *Spatio-temporal dependency constraints between different sensor cloud services.* Services are usually modelled as function calls focusing on their input and output types [160]. However, to model sensor cloud services, we should consider spatio-temporal dependency constraints between services. These constraints may require that the invocation of a sensor cloud service only occurs in the

---

[1]http://sensorcloud.com.

[2]http://www3.ntu.edu.sg/intellisys.

spatio-temporal domain of other sensor cloud services. Therefore, a new spatio-temporal model for sensor cloud services needs to be defined to answer a query by considering all spatio-temporal dependency constraints of sensor cloud services.

- *Spatio-temporal composition model.* The composition provides an elegant means to aggregate sensor cloud services to provide a value-added sensor cloud service. The composition of sensor cloud services is different from classical service composition [66, 106, 141] because of the distributed, volatile and dynamic aspects including *spatio-temporal* dependencies. Spatio-temporal dependency constraints between component sensor cloud services need to be considered in order to compose sensor cloud services. These spatio-temporal constraints may require that the invocation of a sensor cloud service only occurs in the spatio-temporal domain of its dependent sensor cloud services. As a result, a new composition model is required to use the spatio-temporal features of sensor cloud services.

- *A quality model for sensor cloud services.* What distinguishes services from other computing paradigms is their ability to work in a competitive environment where the key parameter to distinguish between similar services is their quality. Knowledge in itself is not sufficient, but needs to be acted upon to bring about benefits. In the case of services, it is the ability to use Quality of Service (QoS) as a key discriminant to choose between services that provide the "action" on knowledge about services [65, 119, 161]. Consequently, non-functional (i.e., QoS) properties need to differentiate candidate sensor cloud services during selection. Existing QoS approaches are not usually based on dynamic environments such as those found in sensed environments. Therefore, we require an extensible QoS model for sensor cloud services that takes into account dynamic features of sensors, especially spatio-temporal characteristics.

- *Spatio-temporal indexing of sensor cloud services.* Indexing available sensor cloud services enables rapid selection of services. Since the underlying sensor cloud services rely on real-time sensor data, a key challenge in indexing is considering the real-time changes of sensor cloud services' behaviour. In addition, indexing sensor cloud services based on spatio-temporal attributes is of paramount importance. Therefore, there needs to be a spatio-temporal index data structure for the efficient access and organization of sensor cloud services.

- *Dynamic reconfiguration of sensor cloud service composition.* Failures need to be addressed since a previously selected sensor cloud service may no longer be available. As a result, the composed service would now be formally deemed to have failed. In such a case, the initial composition plan would need to be replanned to deal with the rising exception. Classical dynamic service reconfig-uration approaches [7, 96, 103] do not consider spatio-temporal dependencies among sensor cloud services. Consequently, we need to devise a spatio-temporal replanning approach for real-time reaction to unavailable sensor cloud services; "unavailable" in the sense they are no longer spatially or temporally available.

- *Spatio-temporal crowdsourcing.* The ubiquity of sensor-enabled mobile devices such as smartphones enables users contributing as multi-modal sensors to collect, analyse and share sensor data [23, 80]. Crowdsourcing [64] is an emerging trend that utilizes contributions from users and the collective wisdom of the crowd [10]. It is important to build a service-based approach to make these crowdsourced sensor cloud data available. This can also be an effective means to enable the crowd to provide a service sharing community within a geographical area by using their smartphones [41]. Users can take advantage of services from their neighbourhood users through this crowdsourced service community. Since the crowd (i.e., service providers) is mobile, the availability of crowdsourced services to users is limited to its spatio-temporal adjacency, i.e., both service providers and users should be within a spatial region at the particular time. A key issue is selecting and composing services from such a large number of ever-changing crowdsourced sensor cloud services to fulfill users' requirements in a real-time fashion and based on spatio-temporal features. As a result, new spatio-temporal service selection and composition technologies are key approaches to leverage spatio-temporal crowdsourcing as a service provisioning platform.

- *Incentivizing crowdsourced providers.* While mobility provides great opportunities to dynamically extend crowdsourced service coverage, it also presents fundamental challenges in terms of service availability to provide users with the best quality of experience when it comes to coverage while on the move in space and time. To achieve desired coverage of services, there is a need to motivate the crowd toward greater participation. Since crowdsourcing is more likely to be used if there are financial rewards and other incentives, an appropriate incentive model is required to motivate service providers to form various types of environment-demanded crowdsourced service distributions.

1.3   Research Objectives

This book investigates and develops a novel framework which effectively and efficiently provide cloud-based crowdsourced sensor data to users in the form of services taking into account the users' spatio-temporal context and QoS requirements. It aims to provide service users the best Quality of Experience (QoE) with a set of composed crowdsourced sensor data-based services. The specific aims of this book are as follows.

- **To design and develop a service framework for cloud-based sensor data.** In this book, we design and develop a service-oriented architecture that provides an integrated view of sensor data shared in the cloud and delivered as sensor cloud services. In this regard, we further identify three secondary aims:

  - *To build a spatio-temporal model for sensor cloud services.* The first task is to model the sensor cloud services which are the building blocks of service architecture. Our spatio-temporal features model these sensor cloud services. The collected cloud-based sensor data will be analysed and abstracted as sensor cloud services to develop the spatio-temporal service model.

- *To devise a new real-time index model to access sensor cloud services.* There is also a need to manage the real-time sensor data exposed as services in the cloud. The second task applies spatio-temporal index data structures for efficient access and organization of sensor cloud services.
- *To develop a quality model for sensor cloud services.* Given the diversity of service offerings, an important challenge for users is to discover the 'right' service satisfying their requirements. In this regard, the third task focuses on a new quality model having the dynamic aspects of sensor cloud services. Quality criteria are part of describing the non-functional aspects (QoS) of sensor cloud services.

- **To devise QoS-aware spatio-temporal composition of sensor cloud services.** Composition is a means to aggregate sensor cloud services to provide new functionalities. This research designs a set of spatio-temporal composition frameworks for sensor cloud services. We investigate the following two secondary aims:

  - *To design an approach for sensor cloud service selection and composition.* This task aims to develop a set of spatio-temporal composition algorithms. Specifically, we first identify the composability model to determine whether two component sensor cloud services are spatio-temporally composable. We then focus on investigating techniques for composing sensor cloud services.
  - *To design a failure-proof model for sensor cloud service composition.* Failures may occur as users follow their optimal composition plans. For example, the QoS of sensor cloud services may fluctuate and a component service may no longer fulfil expectations. As a result, the initial composition plan needs to be repaired. We propose to devise a new incremental replanning algorithm to re-execute the composition at midway when new information about the environment is received.

- **To design a crowdsourcing platform for real-time and adaptive service provisioning.** Crowdsourcing is a cost-effective means for sensor cloud deployment through collecting sensor data from pervasive sensing devices such as smartphones. We aim to leverage crowdsourcing of sensors (e.g., smartphones) as a key mechanism for providing this sensor cloud service. This research objective focuses on modelling the crowdsourced sensor cloud services based on spatio-temporal features. It also includes designing a novel technique to compose crowdsourced services based on users' various functional and QoS requirements. We also explore the use of some heuristics to optimise the selection and composition process.
- **To devise an incentive model to drive coverage of crowdsourced sensor cloud services.** The incentive is a driving mechanism to induce the spatio-temporal movement of crowdsourced sensor cloud service providers to attain the desired coverage. We design and develop a spatio-temporal incentive-based technique to promote the service crowdsourcing and achieve demanded coverage of crowdsourced sensor cloud services within a region.

1.4   Contributions

The specific aim of this research is a novel QoS-based crowdsourced sensor cloud service selection and composition framework using the power of the service paradigm. The details of the contributions are discussed on chapter-by-chapter basis in the following subsections.

1.4.1   A QoS-Aware Framework for Spatio-Temporal Selection and Composition of Sensor Cloud Services

We present a spatio-temporal selection and composition framework for sensor cloud services. We first define a new line segment sensor cloud service model. Spatio-temporal features will be the focal aspects of the service model. In this model, a sensor cloud service consists of a number of functional attributes and associated QoS. In particular, new spatio-temporal QoS attributes are proposed to evaluate sensor cloud services based on spatio-temporal properties of the services. We develop a service organization to efficiently discover sensor cloud services. We propose a spatio-temporal index structure customizing a 3D R-tree to efficiently access sensor cloud services. We also propose a spatio-temporal linear composition algorithm which enables users to select their desired sensor cloud services based on multiple criteria. Our heuristic composition algorithm is a variation of A* shortest path finding algorithm [58] offering an optimal QoS.

Failures also need to be addressed since the QoS of a component sensor cloud service may not always fulfil the expectation. Consequently, the composed service has now formally failed. In this regard, we propose a failure-proof spatio-temporal combinatorial search algorithm for real-time reaction to unavailable sensor cloud services based on the D* Lite algorithm [83]. It is an incremental version of the A* algorithm. Our proposed approach continually improves its initial composition plan while QoS constraints change. We test the proposed composition approaches using a public transport scenario to devise the best public transport journey plan.

1.4.2   Coverage as a Service: Two-Level Composition of Crowdsourced Sensor Cloud Services

We propose a two-level QoS-based crowdsourced sensor cloud service composition framework to select the optimal composite crowdsourced services along a set of optimal linear composition plans using a set of quality parameters. The framework contains a novel service and composition model, quality model and a set of novel techniques to compose crowdsourced sensor cloud services. We first present a new *region* service model which aims to abstract a crowdsourced sensor cloud service focusing on spatio-temporal features. We define the overlay spatio-temporal composability models which check that two component services are spatio-temporally composable. We use the heuristic of path direction to minimize the number of candidate services in the composition process and optimise the selection process. We then propose novel QoS attributes for evaluating crowdsourced services. We introduce a new coverage QoS as a service which is formulated as a composition of crowdsourced services. Finally, we propose a two-level spatio-temporal composition algorithm based on users' functional and non-functional requirements. At the first level, the coverage quality parameter of a line segment service is formulated as the problem of computing an overlay spatio-temporal composition. The second level takes the first level output as a coverage QoS value of a line segment service to select the optimal linear composition plan. A significant aspect is that *the overlay service composition* acts as a QoS of the line segment service composition. We investigate two different approaches to double-layered sensor cloud service composition. We present a set of heuristic algorithms based on the shortest path algorithm like A* and Dijkstra as the basis for finding the optimal linear and overlay composition plan. Our case study focuses on the use of (1) WiFi hotspot sharing and (2) journey planning in a geographical region.

1.4.3 A Novel Spatio-Temporal Incentive-Based Framework for Crowdsourced Services

Finally, we present a new spatio-temporal incentive-based approach to achieve a geographically balanced coverage of crowdsourced services. The incentive model aims to achieve demanded coverage of crowdsourced services by employing a virtual credit mechanism to reward crowdsourced service providers who move to required locations within the required time. The proposed spatio-temporal incentive model differentiates areas with different rewards. This differentiation depends on the spatio-temporal dynamicity of the environment. In this regard, we consider the types of environment based demands, such as spatio-temporal density, time of day, popularity of locations in order to design the incentive model so that crowdsourced service providers can be incentivized according to the environment's demands. The approach aims to provide users with the best QoE by redistributing hotspot coverage within a predefined geographic area. We propose a novel greedy redistribution algorithm that offers incentives to crowdsourced service providers to achieve an optimal demanded coverage. The algorithm tries to reach a coverage equilibrium in an iterative process through assigning crowdsourced service providers in the over-supplied subregions to undersupplied subregions. We introduce a new participation probability model that determines the expected number of crowdsourced service providers for movement. Our case study focuses on the use of WiFi hotspot sharing within any given geographical area.

1.5   Outline of the Book Chapters

The rest of this book is organised as follows.

In Chap. 2, we present an in-depth study of the background of the field and the closely related issues. We start by introducing WSNs, cloud computing and the integration of WSNs and cloud computing, i.e., sensor cloud. We also review previously proposed frameworks to sensor cloud and explains their specific characteristics. We also review the related studies on service composition and discuss previously proposed approaches along with their strengths and shortcomings. Finally, we discuss the related work in the area of spatio-temporal crowdsourcing and incentive models that are most closely related to our research.

In Chap. 3, we propose a service-oriented framework to efficiently and effectively select and compose sensor cloud services. We first introduce the notion of the line segment sensor cloud service model which specifies functional and non-functional (QoS) attributes of sensor data taking into account the spatio-temporal aspects. We develop a model to spatio-temporally index the sensor cloud services. We also propose a selection algorithm to search for and select sensor cloud services. In addition, new quality parameters are defined to evaluate sensor cloud services. In particular, we present a spatio-temporal linear composition approach for finding the optimal composition plan. A new failure-proof spatio-temporal composition algorithm is proposed to deal with any failure of services. Finally, we discuss the experimental results.

In Chap. 4, we propose a two-level spatio-temporal composition algorithm. We first present a formal spatio-temporal model and quality model for a crowdsourced sensor cloud service. We then propose two different approaches to a double-layered crowdsourced sensor cloud service composition: *one path at a time* and *one segment at a time*. Additionally, we develop an overlay composition technique to determine the coverage QoS value of the line segment service that is presented in Chap. 3. We analyse the performance of these approaches through the experiments.

In Chap. 5, we present an incentive-based approach to achieve demanded coverage of crowdsourced sensor cloud services. It also targets changing coverage of the crowdsourced services from the environment-oriented dimensions. First, we introduce a new spatio-temporal incentive model to encourage the spatio-temporal movement of crowdsourced service providers. We also propose a new greedy redistribution algorithm to reach the desired coverage. Finally, we describe the experiments and their results.

In Chap. 6, we summarize the contributions and outcomes of this book. We also discuss directions for future research.

Chapter 2
Background

To the best of our knowledge, there is no similar composition approach in the literature considering spatio-temporal aspects. The strength of the proposed framework is the ability to combine techniques from four separate areas, i.e., sensor cloud, service composition, spatio-temporal crowdsourcing and incentive models. The sensor cloud is a potential key to storing and accessing large-scale sensor data. The concept of services is used as an abstraction that delivers data through the sensor cloud to end-users. In addition, a composition of sensor cloud services creates new value-added functionality to resolve complex sensor cloud service requests. Spatio-temporal features are fundamental to the functional aspect of the sensor cloud. In this regard, we focus on spatio-temporal aspects as key parameters to access sensor cloud services. A credit-based incentive model motivates crowd participation to achieve the desired coverage. In this chapter, we provide an overview of related work in these areas.

The rest of this chapter is organised as follows. We start by presenting the basic history of research activity in the sensor cloud domain in Sect. 2.1. We then present various techniques which are used for service compositions in Sect. 2.2. In Sect. 2.3, we discuss the role of spatio-temporal crowdsourcing. We present previous studies in the domain of incentive models in Sect. 2.4. Finally, we conclude the chapter in Sect. 2.5.

2.1 Sensor Cloud Architecture

The sensor cloud is a new paradigm for processing and analyzing big sensor data using the cloud platform. In this section, we first present a brief overview of Wireless Sensor Networks (WSNs), cloud computing and its integration with WSNs. We finally review the sensor cloud including its definition, architectures and applications.

© Springer International Publishing AG, part of Springer Nature 2018
A. Ghari Neiat, A. Bouguettaya, *Crowdsourcing of Sensor Cloud Services*,
https://doi.org/10.1007/978-3-319-91536-4_2

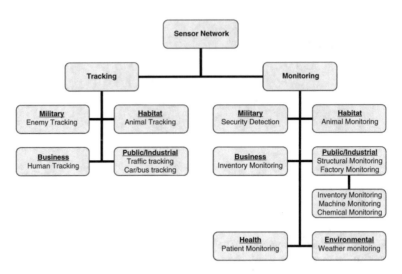

Fig. 2.1 Overview of sensor applications [159]

2.1.1 Wireless Sensor Networks

A typical WSN consists of a number of heterogeneous sensor nodes. Wireless networks of sensor nodes enable monitoring and control of the environment from remote locations. WSNs improve the accuracy of sensing data through collaboration among sensor nodes and online data processing at those nodes [61]. Current WSNs are deployed on land, under-ground, underwater and in space satellites. They are usually designed for specific applications to track the behaviour of the monitored entity or to monitor an environment to take the proper action when necessary. Therefore, these applications can be classified in terms of tracking and monitoring [159] (see Fig. 2.1). Monitoring applications include wildlife monitoring, environmental monitoring (such as weather forecasting), health and wellness monitoring, power monitoring, inventory and factory monitoring. Tracking applications include tracking objects, animals, humans and vehicles. Moreover, application requirements differ in terms of storage, computation and user interface. To meet this diversity of applications, the development of new communication protocols, designs, and services is needed [159].

2.1.2 Cloud Computing

The rapid developments in processing and storage technologies and the success of the Internet have enabled a new computing paradigm called cloud computing, in which on-demand resources (e.g., infrastructure, platform and software) similar to general utilities (e.g., water, electricity and gas) are rapidly provided and released [166]. The core features of the cloud computing include virtualized resources, elastic resource capacity, programmable self-service interface and pay-per-use pricing models [94].

There are four types of cloud deployment models [107]:

Public Cloud: This is the most common form of cloud computing, in which the cloud is made available on a pay-as-you-go basis to the general public [13]. It is owned by an organization selling cloud services. These services are accessible over the Internet via Web applications or Web services from an off-site third-party provider sharing computing resources with many customers [74]. Public clouds are run by third parties and applications from different customers who are likely to be mixed together on the cloud's servers, storage systems or networks [51]. Some popular examples of public clouds include Amazon Elastic Cloud Compute, Google App Engine and Microsoft Azure.

Private Cloud: The private cloud infrastructure is provided for the exclusive use of one business or one organization which has full control over the applications it runs and also over the people and organisations using it. Private clouds can be managed by the organization or a third party service provider. In addition, it may exist on or off premises. The main advantage of the private cloud is using all advantages of virtualization while retaining control over its infrastructure [136]. Google Gmail and Google Apps are well-known examples of services supported by a private cloud infrastructure [30].

Hybrid Cloud: The hybrid cloud infrastructure is a composite of two or more types of clouds (private and public). Companies in hybrid clouds can benefit from scalable resources in the public cloud while keeping data or specific applications within their private cloud. Hybrid clouds can take a number of forms, including cloud-bursting [118], where an organization uses its own computing infrastructure for normal usage. However, in the case of a temporarily heavy workload, it is dynamically extended from a private cloud to an external public cloud service (such as Salesforce) to handle additional computing requirements.

Community Cloud: The cloud infrastructure is shared by several organizations with similar requirements which can share their infrastructures such as data and computing resources through defined interfaces. It may be considered to be a generalization of a private cloud as an infrastructure which is only accessible by one certain organization. For example, all government organizations within the State of California may share computing infrastructure in the cloud to manage data related to its citizens in California.

2.1.2.1 Cloud Services

A cloud delivers computing resources to users as services on an on-demand basis. Clouds, in general, provide services at three different levels as follows [107, 147] (see Fig. 2.2).

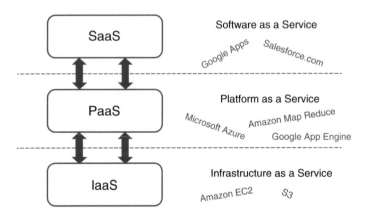

Fig. 2.2 The three layers of cloud computing [147]

Software as a Service (SaaS) delivers simple software programs, applications and customer interface to end users through a web portal in a pay-per-use manner. Therefore, the users can access the on-line software services offering the same functionality instead of installing software on their own computers. SaaS alleviates the troubles of software deployment and maintenance. Moreover, it simplifies development and testing for service providers. For example, Salesforce is an industry leader in providing online CRM (Customer Relationship Management) Services [51].

Platform as a Service (PaaS) provides a platform to support the entire application and service life cycle including design, development, testing, monitoring, deployment and hosting on the cloud with no need to download and install software. There are some restrictions for developers on the type of software they can write in exchange for built-in application scalability [51]. Three typical examples of PaaS are Microsoft Azure, Amazon Map Reduce and Google App Engine: they enable users to build Web applications on the same scalable systems that power Google applications.

Infrastructure as a Service (IaaS) provides hardware, software and equipment to deliver software application environments with a resource usage-based pricing model. Infrastructure can dynamically scale up and down based on application resource requirements. IaaS providers normally offer virtualized infrastructure as a service instead of selling raw hardware infrastructures. Virtualization enables abstraction and encapsulation of hardware level resources. Typical examples are Amazon EC2 (Elastic Cloud Computing) Service and S3 (Simple Storage Service).

Cloud services also play a significant role in sensing and monitoring as they provide powerful computing resources and elastic resource capacities which are not yet available on small sensor devices themselves.

2.1.3 Sensor Cloud

The large amount of real-time sensor data streaming from WSNs pose significant challenges because of specific needs in storage capacity, processing power, energy and data management constraints [9, 159]. To address these challenges, new powerful and scalable computing platforms are needed. Cloud computing is a promising technology providing virtualized resources, elastic resource capacity, programmable self-service interface and pay-per-use pricing models [94]. Therefore, cloud computing is a promising solution that addresses WSNs challenges [95, 154]. The integration of WSNs with the cloud (i.e., sensor cloud) provides unique capabilities and opportunities, particularly for the use of data service-centric applications [123]. Sensor cloud is a potential key to enable large-scale data sharing and cooperation among different users and applications. In what follows, we discuss several challenges enabling sensor cloud in details.

Scalability. The promising applications of WSNs have posed new challenges. For example, the frequency of sampling data in WSNs including seismic sensors or bio-sensors can increase significantly if a situation becomes worse [99, 100]. A large amount of sampled data increases the need for more storage capacity. However, WSNs have their shortcomings to scale well in large networks. Therefore, an elastic storage mechanism is necessary to satisfy storage constraints and data loss prevention requirements. A cloud can provide elastic storage resources to address this issue.

Processing. Some applications such as environmental monitoring and modelling applications have unpredictable computational demands [95]. On the other hand, current WSNs are not able to provide the powerful analytical resources needed to satisfy such requirements. Moreover, cloud computing can elastically provide missing computing capability. In particular, as collected sensor data is often stored and processed off-line, cloud can supply continuous running on-line algorithms to analyse sensor data [99].

Reusability. WSNs provide valuable information to make critical decisions. There are many reasons for maintaining sensed information including historical, future resources and reanalysis [5]. In contrast, the cost of managing and maintaining these sensor resources is a key shortcoming for WSNs, specifically for short life-cycle applications [95]. As a result, sensed information will be deleted quickly after that application no longer requires it. To reuse sensed information for further processing, unlimited data storage of cloud can be a feasible solution.

Availability. WSNs are used by their specific applications for a specific purpose [9]. Each application manages its own physical sensors and sensor data which cannot be used by other applications' users [163]. To share WSN resources among different kinds of applications, lightweight virtualization technologies are required [94]. The cloud computing platform is a promising approach to promote data sharing within existing WSNs.

Reliability. In a WSN, there is normally one server (single point of failure) in operation that can fail at any time due to hardware, software and communication issues. If the server becomes unavailable, sensor data will be inaccessible [100].

Consequently, it is necessary to provide disaster recovery and data backup services to handle failures before and after they occur [159]. Cloud can provide a backup system in case of failure of the main server through geographically distributed data centres [99].

Research in sensor cloud has mainly focused on the integration of WSNs with the cloud. For example, [162] proposes a new sensor cloud architecture which establishes multiple physical sensors as virtual sensors on the cloud. Virtualization provides an abstraction layer for the user as if the user interacts with the physical sensors directly without worrying about the physical sensor location. In [59], a framework for the integration of sensor network and the cloud is proposed through adapting a content-based publish/subscribe platform [47] that simplifies this integration. In the content-based publish/subscribe system, the meta-data has to be added to sensor data to identify the different data fields. In this framework, sensor data is transferred to a publish/subscribe broker, located on the cloud side, through a gateway. This broker delivers information to the cloud consumers. A mechanism is proposed in [91] to transfer sensor data from sensor nodes to the cloud. This sensor-clod mechanism filters the collected data using sensors at the sensor gateway through applying trained neural networks for anomaly detection. The compressed sensor data is sent to the cloud gateway where the data is first decompressed and then uploaded to the cloud. In [109], a theoretical model for virtualization is presented, which is a key enabler of the sensor cloud. A comparative performance study between the sensor cloud and WSN in terms of energy consumption, fault tolerance, lifetime of a sensor node and cost effectiveness is shown in [109]. The results present that the sensor cloud outperforms traditional WSNs in most cases. In [102], the sensor cloud is defined as a cloud of virtual sensors built on top of physical wireless sensors to provide sensing as a service to the user. A three-layer sensor cloud architecture from the Missouri University of Science and Technology is also presented (see Fig. 2.3). The architecture consists of three layers: client-centric, middleware and sensor-centric. Client-centric acts as a gateway to connect users to a sensor cloud. It also allows users to specify their own parameters including regions of interest, sensing phenomena, sampling frequency and sensing duration. The middleware layer provides an intermediary for data communication between client-centric and sensor-centric layers. It also negotiates between the user and the sensor cloud for virtual sensor provisioning for each incoming request and maintenance of virtual sensors. The sensor-centric layer deals directly with physical wireless sensors through the WSN registration, WSN maintenance and data collection components. Sensing and Actuation as a Service (SAaaS) [43] is a cloud of sensors and actuators. Its key functionalities include enabling of interoperation and management of WSNs, smartphones and other devices equipped with sensors and/or actuators in a cloud environment, exploitation of volunteer-based methods for enrolling, aggregating and managing virtual sensors and actuators. The sensing as a service [121] framework enables sensor data to be published and makes that data available to consumers through the cloud either for free or for a fee. In this framework, consumers are allowed to select the number of sensors they require, based on the context information. For example, a user may be willing to pay more for highly accurate sensor data.

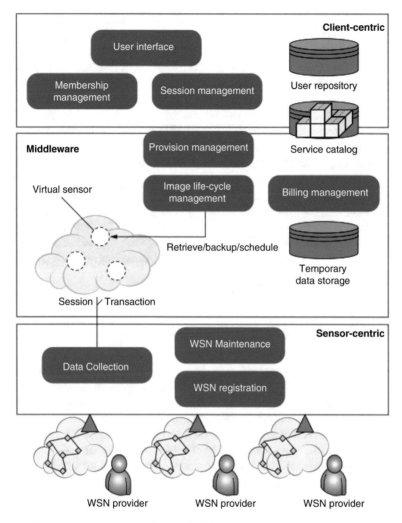

Fig. 2.3 A layered sensor cloud architecture [102]

The sensor cloud enables several new real-life applications including health-care, transport monitoring, target tracking, disaster management, agriculture, environmental monitoring and power management [35]. For example, BodyCloud [50] is a sensor cloud system developed for integrating sensor data collected from Body Sensor Networks (BSNs) with the cloud infrastructure. The system is a SaaS architecture that supports a scalable data management, processing and analysis. The system enables large-scale data sharing and collaborations among users and applications in the cloud. To address security perspectives, a secure and scalable e-health sensor cloud whose objective is managing a large amount of generated data by medical WSNs and dynamically scaling resources through on-demand provisioning is proposed in [100]. A fine-grained access control with low computation overhead that combines Ciphertext Policy Attribute Based Encryption (CPABE) [17] and symmetric encryption is used to ensure data security and confidentiality. In [32], the design and implementation of a sensor cloud to manage and monitor collected sensor data, such as humidity and temperature from an agriculture system is described. A sensor cloud architecture is proposed in [19] that enables on-demand and shared access by users to multiple physical sensors from different applications including healthcare and environment monitoring through virtual sensors. [26] addresses the problem of correctly mapping sensors to targets in target tracking applications within a sensor cloud environment. The main contribution is proposing a dynamic mapping algorithm based on the theory of social choice [20] to ensure the fair and best allocation of sensors to their corresponding targets. That work is extended in [110] by proposing a new QoS-aware sensor allocation approach, taking into account QoS parameters such as detection probability, dwelling time and availability. The proposed selection process is also an auction-based mechanism that ensures a balance between the QoS and the cost incurred by the user.

2.1.4 Sensor Cloud Service Framework

A key challenge in the sensor cloud is the efficient delivery of sensor data to end users. The preferred paradigm and abstraction is services to transform data into useful information, i.e., sensor data is made available as a service (aka sensor cloud service) to different clients over a sensor cloud infrastructure [35]. There have been little research into the sensor cloud which focuses on a service-oriented architecture to abstract the functionality of sensor data as a service. For example, [163] develops a sensor cloud service model which provides service instances (virtual sensors) to end users (see Fig. 2.4). Users request services according to their own needs by selecting an appropriate service template of the sensor cloud. [8] proposes a virtualized Internet of Things (IoT) framework called Sensor-as-a-Service (SenaaS). This framework exposes the functional aspects of sensors as services through hiding details from the user. SenaaS mainly focuses on providing sensor management as a service rather than sensor data provisioning (collection and dissemination) as a service. The framework comprises three layers: (a) the real-world access layer, providing an interface with an underlying IoT cloud to overcome the technical diversity in terms of sensor types and communication mechanisms; (b) the semantic overlay layer, adding semantic annotations to the sensor configuration process through maintaining an IoT ontology, a sensor ontology, an event ontology and service access policies, and (c) the service virtualization layer, abstracting functional aspects of an underlying IoT cloud and exposing information in the form of services to facilitate users. A similar approach is presented by [67] where sensors are encapsulated to a service with semantic annotations. They also propose a model-based approach based on UML Activity diagrams and their associated semantics

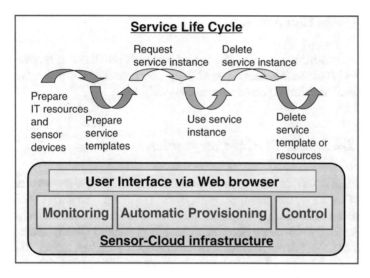

Fig. 2.4 Overview of sensor cloud infrastructure [163]

for the efficient sensor service discovery and composition. Not only does our work contribute to the integration of WSNs and the cloud, but also our service model is different from other sensor cloud service models which focus on spatio-temporal features.

There is a number of services and middlewares on the sensor cloud infrastructure which collect, share and process sensor data on the cloud. We briefly describe few of them. Nimbits [1] is a social data service that provides data compression, data calculation and alert management on collected sensor data. Pachube [2] provides a platform that enables users to collect, store, share and discover real-time sensor data in different areas including healthcare, environment and energy. These services have some limitations in terms of sensor data management and interoperability among services from different sensor data resources [9]. Hydra [45] is middleware consisting of an intelligent software layer placed between the operating system and applications. Global Sensor Networks (GSN) [4] is an evolving middleware for sensor data stream processing. GSN also rapidly simplifies the process of connecting heterogeneous sensor devices to applications. Specifically, GSN provides the capability to integrate, discover, combine, query and filter sensor data through a declarative XML-based language and enables zero-programming deployment and management. The virtual sensor is the key element in the GSN. Virtual sensors in GSN are defined using XML, whereas approaches such as [78] where virtual sensors are defined based on classes,. Additionally, Hydra and GSN are data-centric frameworks. They provide services as an API to access data. In contrast, our approach is service-centric. We consider services as first class objects to query and access.

2.2   Service Composition

Service composition is one of the hottest research problems in service-oriented computing [106]. In this section, we briefly overview the principal related works of traditional, mobile and timed service compositions.

2.2.1   Traditional Service Composition

The traditional service composition problem can be categorized into two areas. The first focuses on the functional composability among component services. The second area aims to compose optimal services based on non-functional properties (QoS). Functional-driven service composition approaches typically adopt semantic descriptions of services. Examples of automatic approaches include the policy-based approach proposed in [31] and the composability model driven approach proposed in [106]. Functional-driven service composition approaches do not generally attempt to find an optimal solution but instead focus on finding a solution. The QoS of the resulting composite service are usually used as a determinant factor to ensure users' satisfaction. Different users may have different requirements and preferences regarding QoS. Therefore, QoS-aware composition approaches are required. The QoS-aware service composition problem is usually modelled as a Multiple Criteria Decision Making [164] problem. The most popular approaches include integer linear programming and genetic algorithms. An Integer Linear Program (ILP) consists of a set of variables, a set of linear constraints and a linear objective function. After translating the composition problem into this formalism, a specific solver software such as LPSolve can be used. [24] and [158] use Genetic Algorithms (GA) for service composition. There are also some service composition algorithms [73, 117, 155] which apply A* shortest path finding algorithm to find the optimal composition plan. Most classical composition techniques are off-line and are mostly inapplicable for composing services using dynamic features [46] such as those found in sensor cloud applications. Those works on traditional service composition form the background of our research. We recast the problem into QoS-aware service composition problem and utilize an extension of A* algorithm to find the optimal composition plan. However, we model the service composition problem in a sensor cloud environment taking into account spatio-temporal features which are not easy to apply in traditional methods.

2.2.2   Mobile Service Composition

Recent advances in smart mobile devices have enabled more powerful mobile applications and services that were not previously available on desktops or laptops. As a result, more studies have emerged to address the problem of mobile service composition that is more flexible and complex than traditional service compositions

[39]. [128] proposes a mobile service composition algorithm in opportunistic networks that allow mobile users to benefit from a larger set of services available in the local environment. They also present an efficient service selection algorithm for devices located in close proximity considering the service load and temporal distances between nodes of the composition graph. Temporal distance provides a measure for reachability of nodes (i.e., the relative location of other nodes) when an end-to-end connected path does not exist. For each node, the service composition graph builds a local view of the services available at other nodes. The vertices of the composition graph are nodes and edges represent the cost of obtaining a certain service from that node. This mobile composition algorithm selects a composition sequence based on the composition graph to meet the user's requirements. [153] incorporates a mobility prediction approach into the dependable service composition in wireless mobile ad hoc networks. The mobility prediction helps to determine the estimated time that a service provider is available in the current environment instead of predicting its future location. It aims to find an optimal service composition that has maximum tolerance to the uncertainty of the mobility prediction. This provides a more reliable composition in terms of mobility. It also assumes that the execution duration of each service is the same on every provider. This assumption is not reasonable in real life because of different hardware configurations of service providers. This work mainly focuses on the impact of mobility of service providers on reliability. However, none of the approaches in [153] and [128] take into account QoS properties to find the optimal composition plan. [41] introduces a new mobile provisioning architecture called Mobile Service Sharing Community (MSSC) where both service requesters and providers are moving. They propose a mobility model that is an extension of Random WayPoint (RWP) model [75] for abstracting users' moving behaviour. This mobility model also assumes that users can only travel among a number of critical points which limits its usefulness. They also propose a service composition approach based on Krill-Herd algorithm [54] to find the optimal response time. A QoS-aware mobility-aware service composition algorithm is proposed in [38]. They introduce the concept of mobility-aware QoS based on the mobility model of service invocations that describes the performance of a service. Due to the changes in location and mobile network strength, the data transmission time changes which affects the response time. On the other hand, [41] and [38] approaches only consider the location sensitive response time as a QoS criterion to select the optimal composition plan. [116] develops a QoS-aware service composition model to handle the mobile environment. This model is based on traditional QoS criteria and a new dynamic QoS criterion (i.e., availability) which reflects the mobility. They also introduce a k-neighbour algorithm which decomposes the composite service into smaller elementary composite services. Each such service includes at most k consecutive atomic services. This algorithm finds the composition plan for those elementary composite services based on the available service provider set. GoCoMo [28] is a self-organizing, goal-driven service composition model in mobile and pervasive computing environments. It introduces a decentralized heuristic planning algorithm based on the backward-chaining to support a flexible service query. A risk-aware

mobile service composition algorithm is proposed in [40] to deal with the risk of failures resulting from the mobility of service consumers and providers. This service composition approach is a modification of the simulated annealing algorithm [148] to find the optimal mobile composite service that has the best QoS and lower risk. Too little attention has been paid to sensor cloud service composition particularly in terms of *spatio-temporal* features. Our work considers QoS constraints and both spatial and temporal dependencies among services.

2.2.3   *Timed Service Composition*

Some works have taken temporal properties into consideration to select the optimal service composition. For example, [56] augments the behaviour of Web services with time properties. This mechanism is based on a timed mediator to deal with the problem of timed (and non-timed) conflicts when generating an asynchronous Web service composition. Time-dependent and input-dependent QoS attributes (i.e., execution time and inter-domain validation) are considered in [167] to compose services in multi-domain environments. The service composition is also modelled as the multi-domain scheduling problem. Moreover, [150] defines a multi-objective optimization-based approach while considering time-dependent QoS values. In this approach, a time-dependent pricing model is also used to show how time and input aspects affect the QoS values of a service. For example, the price of a movie service may differ depending on the time of viewing (e.g., weekends, weekdays or release date). It selects the best combination of services while specifying the start and finish times of each service according to the QoS values at each time period. To address timed service composition problem, an approach is proposed in [82] which considers time-dependent QoS attributes to select best service instances. There is also an assumption that all QoS attributes are monotonically decreasing. [42] proposes a differential evolutionary approach for constraints-driven service composition problem satisfying both QoS and temporal constraints in mobile cloud computing. This approach also takes into account the service provider mobility which is modelled by extending the proposed mobility model in [153]. A pruning mechanism for service selection is presented in [57] that considers time-dependent QoS attributes associated with temporal constraints. The QoS values of these composition approaches depend on the time of execution. In contrast, our work goes beyond existing approaches by considering both time-dependent and location-dependent QoS; i.e., QoS values of a service are affected by the locations and times of services.

2.3   Spatio-Temporal Crowdsourced Services

In this section, we overview related works in the area of spatio-temporal crowdsourcing and crowdsourced service composition.

2.3.1 Spatio-Temporal Crowdsourcing

The ubiquity of sensor-enabled mobile devices such as smartphones enables public and professional users contributing as multi-modal sensors to collect, analyse and share sensor data including location, time, direction and acceleration [23, 80]. Crowdsourcing [64] can be a means to utilize the contributions from users and the collective wisdom of the crowd [10]. Since the crowd (i.e., sensors) is mobile, the produced data by the crowd is spatio-temporal. In particular, *spatial* crowdsourcing [10, 80] distributes spatial tasks to a set of so-called crowd workers travelling to specified locations to perform the tasks. For example, [29] deploys CrowdSensing@Place (CSP) framework which combines spatial sensor data (i.e., locations) and user trajectories along with sampled images and audio clips to link place visits with place categories (e.g., restaurants). A new approach for crowdsourcing location-based queries is proposed in [22]. It uses new location-based services such as Foursquare to select an appropriate user for answering the given query. Historical Foursquare check-ins are used instead of assigning spatial tasks to the users. However, only a few studies have focused on spatio-temporal crowdsourcing [105]. [133] presents a crowdsourcing urban simulation to detect a user transportation mode through collecting spatio-temporal data (i.e., date, time and network-based location values) and acceleration sensors values. Mobile crowdsourcing systems are proposed in [168] and [137] to predict real-time arrival of buses using GPS traces of commuters. Further, [49] develops OneBusAway system, consisting of a set of transit tools to provide real-time arrival of buses. OneBusAway enables users to comment through several feedback mechanisms including Twitter, blog and bug tracker. Analyzing such multi-modal and diversified crowdsourced sensed data poses new challenges when it is collected and stored. As a result, we investigate the spatio-temporal crowdsourced sensor cloud services which combine the spatio-temporal crowdsourcing with the sensor cloud to provide more efficient techniques for collecting and processing spatio-temporal sensor data.

2.3.2 Crowdsourced Service Composition

Our work embodies the concept of the spatio-temporal crowdsourcing to design a crowdsourced sensor cloud service framework for a smart city where smartphone users contribute as service providers. Only a few work [68, 79, 113] studied crowdsourcing as a service. For example, [132] introduces sensing as a service (S^2aaS) which is a crowdsourcing system to provide sensing services using mobile phones through a cloud computing system. In this regard, not only a mobile phone user can be a cloud (service) user who requests sensing services but also a mobile service provider who fulfills sensing tasks according to sensing requests from other mobile phone users in different locations [131].

Several researchers have started working on crowdsourced service composition because of the potential of crowdsourced service framework. An agent-based crowd service framework is proposed in [120], which provides crowd intelligence and labor as services (i.e., Web services) through mobile crowdsourcing. A composition approach is also introduced to compose crowdsourced services and computational service considering users' constraints including the cost and response time. The proposed framework is presented by a scenario of purchasing a secondhand laptop. In this scenario, there are two different types of services: (1) an online bank transaction service as a computational service and (2) a crowdsourced site inspection service which checks the site's description validity and crowdsourced price assessment which checks the price as crowdsourced services. For each invocation of a crowdsourced service, the framework launches a crowdsourcing task and selects the workers based on their attributes (e.g., location and service provision records) to perform the task. The selected workers are assigned to their tasks and submit their results. The results are then aggregated into an output result of a composite service. However, this work does not take QoS parameters into account to select the optimal composition plan.

2.4 Incentive Models

Designing effective incentive schemes is an active research area in crowdsourced sensing systems. [157] considers two system models: platform-centric and user-centric. In the platform-centric model, the service provider offers a fixed price to motivate a set of participating users. They model an incentive approach as a Stackelberg game [53] to assign tasks where the sensing cost of each participant is assumed to be known by all other participants. Alternatively, in the user-centric incentive mechanism, a user announces a reserve price which is the lowest price for their participation. The service provider then selects a subset of winning users based on their submitted bids for particular tasks and determines the price payable to each winner. They model a user-centric incentive approach as a reverse auction [89] to price and allocate the sensing tasks where the sensing cost of each user is known only to itself. The above task allocation problem is generalised in [88] by taking into account different participation levels (i.e., the number of sensing samples per unit time) and quality of service delivered to users as the quality of their previously contributed data. They also propose an incentive mechanism based on an optimal reverse auction model [114] that minimizes the total payment to participating users while delivering a certain quality of service to requested users. [93] introduces Reverse Auction-based Dynamic Price (RADP) incentive mechanism where participating users send their claimed bid prices to a service provider and those with the lowest incentive expectations are selected as winners to sell their sensor data. The drawback of this mechanism is that the users who contribute higher true valuations may frequently become starved and drop out of the reverse auction. [92] overcomes this issue by introducing a virtual participant credit (VPC) and a new mechanism, called RADP-VPC. RADP-VPC considers a specific virtual credit as a reward is given to participants who lost in the previous reverse auction only for their participation. As a result, the users with higher true valuations can win by continuously participating. Unlike those reverse auction approaches that allocate a sensing task based only on the negotiated price, Multi-Attribute Auction (MAA) [90] integrates different quality parameters including the amount of submitted data, sensing location distance, location accuracy, the number of previously lost auction rounds and user credibility, in addition to price. A utility function is also applied to reflect the overall value of sensed data based on its attributes. SenseUtil [144] is a participation-aware incentive model leveraging the concept of microeconomics where the supply and demand are incorporated into the value of sensed data. The incentive value depends on several parameters including sensing frequency, travel distance and reward which dynamically change subject to spatio-temporal contexts. [152] optimizes SenseUtil to avoid unnecessary energy and bandwidth consumption at the server end. The optimized SenseUtil is based on a new directional distribution method in which only the participating user whose distance from the point of interest (POI) is less than a distance threshold is selected to do the sensing tasks.

The above works focus on pricing modules (e.g., fixed, bidding or geo-location based) and rewarding mechanisms (e.g., QoS). Another cluster of literature that is closely related to our work focuses on incentive models for improving the coverage of crowdsourced sensed tasks. There are several studies that address the problem of the geographically unbalanced price and coverage of the crowdsourcing [48, 71, 124]. For example, a Greedy Incentive Algorithm (GIA) is proposed in [70], which is a combination of the RADP-VPC mechanism [92] and Greedy Budgeted Maximum Coverage (GBMC) algorithm [81]. GIA selects a set of users according to their location to achieve the lowest cost within a given fixed budget while improving the coverage of the area of interest. It also considers that users are not static i.e., they are moving from local to new regions. [69] extends their GIA algorithm by introducing a SPREAD algorithm which also takes into account the spread of sensors. This algorithm first selects the set of samples that covers all users at minimum cost considering the budget constraints. It then selects the samples that maximize the variance. [92] proposes a model that encourages the movement to new target areas by sending a new offer to participants located close to those areas. [108] proposes the use of a density map which estimates the number of participants per region based on their locations to reconstruct variables of interest in different regions. The density map is utilized by the incentive model to encourage the movement of participants in particular regions. However, these studies are not directly applicable to our work because they do not consider the temporal aspect to reach a coverage balance of participants. Our work takes into account both the spatial and temporal dynamic nature of participants to design an effective incentive model. Few works have addressed the spatio-temporal coverage problem. [139] proposes a spatio-temporal incentive scheme with demand awareness. The approach is modelled based on the spatio-temporal neighbouring contributions and the sensing coverage region. This model encourages participation and selects a representative set of participants which can provide the demanded coverage. However, this approach does not consider redistribution of participants to achieve a balanced coverage within a region.

2.5   Chapter Summary

In this chapter, we have provided a broad overview of the important and relevant topics in relation to the spatio-temporal composition of sensor cloud services, together with a description of their characteristics. We presented a more detailed review of the existing sensor cloud architectures and sensor cloud service frameworks. We then reviewed previous studies on service composition. Finally, we surveyed spatio-temporal crowdsourcing techniques and incentive models proposed in the literature. In this book, we propose approaches to compose sensor cloud services based on spatio-temporal features and to incentivize the service providers to achieve required coverage of crowdsourced services. In Chap. 3, we discuss the spatio-temporal composition of sensor cloud services and how we model them. Section 4.1 will discuss how to leverage spatio-temporal crowdsourcing to introduce a new crowdsourced QoS coverage as a service. Chapter 5 proposes a framework for incentivizing the crowd to participate such that they can provide a balanced crowdsourced coverage.

Chapter 3
Spatio-Temporal Linear Composition
of Sensor Cloud Services

3.1 Introduction

In this chapter, we propose a service-oriented sensor cloud architecture that provides
an integrated view of the sensor data shared on the cloud and delivered as services.
Spatio-temporal features are fundamental to the functional aspect of the sensor
cloud. In this regard, such aspects are key parameters to design a sensor cloud
service framework.

The major contribution of this chapter is that it proposes a novel QoS-based sensor cloud service composition framework using the power of the service paradigm.
Two major components are involved in this framework. The *first* component is a
sensor cloud service management framework that comprises a service model and
an indexing model of sensor cloud services. Therefore, we present a new service
model which aims to abstract a sensor cloud service by conceptualizing the spatio-
temporal aspect of the service as its functional attributes and the qualitative aspects
of the service as its non-functional attributes. The indexing model aims to spatio-
temporally index sensor cloud services to enable an effective and efficient search
of the services. We also define novel QoS attributes for evaluating sensor cloud
services based on dynamic features of the sensor cloud. The composition combines
sensor cloud services to provide a new sensor cloud service. Therefore, the *second*
component of the proposed framework is a spatio-temporal linear composition
algorithm which enables users to select optimal composition plans based on their
own functional and non-functional requirements. Our linear composition algorithm
is a variation of A* shortest path finding algorithm [58] offering an optimal QoS.
In a highly dynamic environment such as is found in sensed environments, the
non-functional properties (QoS) of sensor cloud services may fluctuate [101]. For
example, a participant service may no longer be available or its QoS constraint
has fluctuated at runtime. As a result, the service may no longer provide the
required QoS and so fail. Therefore, the initial composition plan may become non-
optimal and needs to be replanned to deal with the changing conditions of such

© Springer International Publishing AG, part of Springer Nature 2018
A. Ghari Neiat, A. Bouguettaya, *Crowdsourcing of Sensor Cloud Services*,
https://doi.org/10.1007/978-3-319-91536-4_3

environments. We propose an efficient failure-proof spatio-temporal composition algorithm based on the D* Lite algorithm [83] for real-time reaction to unavailable services because they are no longer spatially or temporally available where they were supposed to be. Our proposed approach continually improves its initial composition plan and finds the best composition plan from a given source point to a given destination point while QoS constraints change. We evaluate the proposed composition approaches using a public transport scenario to devise the "best" public transport journey plan. We conduct preliminary experiments to demonstrate the scalability and performance of our proposed approach.

The rest of this chapter is organised as follows. Section 3.2 highlights the related work. Section 3.3 presents the proposed spatio-temporal model for sensor cloud services. Section 3.4 describes the proposed selection process and indexing model. Section 3.5 illustrates the spatio-temporal QoS model. Section 3.6 elaborates the details of the proposed linear composition approach. Section 3.7 details the failure-proof composition approach. Section 3.8 evaluates the proposed approaches and shows the experiment results. Section 3.9 concludes the chapter.

3.1.1 Motivating Scenario

We use a scenario from public transport as our motivating scenario to illustrate the proposed service-oriented sensor cloud architecture. Suppose Sarah is planning to travel from 'A' to 'B'. She wants to get information about the travel services (i.e., buses, trams and trains) in the city to plan her journey. Different users may have different requirements and preferences regarding QoS. For example, Sarah may specify her requirements as a maximum walk of 300 m and waiting time of 10 min at any connecting stop. In this scenario, we assume that each bus (tram / train) has a set of deployed sensors (see Fig. 3.1). It is also assumed that there are several bus sensor providers (i.e., *sensor data providers*) who supply sensor data collected from different buses. We assume each *sensor data provider* owns a subset of a set of sensors on each bus. For example, in Melbourne, Yarra Trams[1] uses intelligent sensors to collect real-time sensor data.

We assume that there are several *sensor cloud data providers* who supply IaaS [13], i.e., CPU services, storage services, and network services to *sensor data providers*. The *sensor cloud data providers* are in charge of delivering the sensor cloud infrastructure services. *Sensor cloud service providers* make query services available so that a user may query multiple heterogeneous *sensor data providers*. We assume that each *sensor cloud service provider* offers one or more sensor cloud services to help commuters devise the "best" journey plan. Different *sensor cloud service providers* may query the same *sensor data providers*. The quality of services is assumed to be different. In our scenario, Sarah uses the sensor cloud services to plan her journey. It is quite possible that a single service cannot satisfy Sarah's

---

[1]http://www.yarratrams.com.au/.

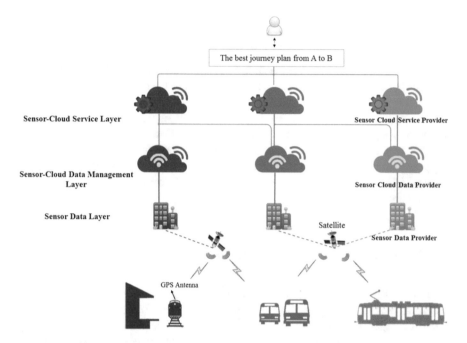

Fig. 3.1 Public transport scenario

requirements. In such cases, sensor cloud services need to be composed to provide the best travel plan from 'A' to 'B'. We reformulate the research problem as follows: What is the optimal path from point 'A' to point 'B' that provides the best QoS based on a user's requirements including maximum waiting time or maximum walk between two stops.

3.2 Background

In this section, we review the main related works in the area of spatio-temporal travel planning, spatio-temporal index methods, dynamic service reconfiguration and replanning algorithms.

3.2.1 Spatio-Temporal Travel Planning

There is a large body of work in spatio-temporal aspects addressing travel planning issues [52, 146]. [55] proposes a model to represent a spatio-temporal network and a shortest-path algorithm based on a time aggregated graph for a fixed start time.

[151] presents a mobility-oriented spatio-temporal data model for activity-based transport. The model supports queries from spatio-temporal and activity-based perspectives. The common denominator in the above work is that they take a data-driven approach to address the research issue. In contrast, our work explores a new area in spatio-temporal travel planning by abstracting the problem using the service paradigm. The use of the service paradigm enables querying a journey map at a higher level of abstraction as users typically think in terms of journey services. Therefore, a journey plan would consist of composing a set of journey services on the map according to a set of functional and non-functional attributes. The proposed service-based approach enables lay users to use any complex multimodal transportation systems while expressing their own constraints (e.g., maximum waiting time).

3.2.2 Spatio-Temporal Index Methods

The capability of providing an efficient access and organization of services and tracking their changes over time is a demanding task. Indexing structures have been leveraged to enable the fast discovery of services. To index services, we should consider spatio-temporal aspects of services. Many tree structures have been extended to support time as a temporal dimension on R-tree [115]. Spatio-temporal index structures have two main categories [111]: (1) indexing based on the *past* position of moving objects including HR-tree [115], 3DR-tree [143] and MV3R-tree [142], and (2) indexing based on the *current* and *future* movement of objects including 2-3TR-tree [3], TPR-tree [129] and ANR-tree [27]. We model services based on historical spatio-temporal sensor data, i.e., the first category. Among the indexing data structures for historical sensor data, HR-tree and 3DR-tree aim at the range query while the others are suitable for the trajectory query. The 3DR-tree adds time as another dimension and represents two-dimensional rectangles with time interval as three-dimensional boxes [104]. The HR-tree maintains a separate R-tree for each time stamp. An R-tree is created whenever an object in a previous R-tree changes. Because of node replication in case of only small changes in data, the HR-tree is not space efficient [104]. Since the 3D R-tree has no duplicate data, the size of the 3D R-tree is significantly smaller than the size of the HR-tree [77]. We assume that the value of *space* of a service rarely changes over the life time of a service while the value of the *time* attribute is continuously changing.

3.2.3 Dynamic Reconfiguration

There are several dynamic reconfiguration approaches to deal with QoS changes at runtime. Most existing approaches have mainly focused on two techniques: *Replacement* and *Re-composition*. *Replacement* approaches aim to replace an affected service with a new service being compatible with composition at runtime [96]. Examples of replacement approaches include one-to-one service mapping [103] and many-to-one service mapping [127]. None of those aforementioned approaches ensure the correctness of reconfiguration after the replacement. [96] applies service behavioural types to guarantee the one-to-one service replacement. Runtime *Re-composition* has been extensively studied [7, 25]. Some examples of re-composition approaches include the end-to-end QoS constraints presented in [98, 165]. None of those dynamic service reconfiguration approaches consider spatio-temporal dependencies among services. In this chapter, we focus on spatio-temporal replanning of the service composition at runtime.

3.2.4 Dynamic Replanning

The A* algorithm has been extensively applied to solve the problem of shortest path planning. Several extensions to A* have been proposed to adapt it to the dynamic environments requiring real-time replanning including *incremental, anytime* and *real-time* [125]. *Incremental* replanning algorithms including D* [138], LPA* [86] and D* Lite reuse information obtained from previous iterations to improve the search instead of recomputing the search from the beginning. *Anytime* algorithms including Anytime D* [97] provide a fast but *non-optimal* plan considering time constraints for finding the solution. In *real-time* algorithms including LRTA* [87] and RTAA* [85], like *anytime*, finding the plan within the time constraint is more important than finding the optimal plan. We use D* Lite which can continually find the optimal plan. D* Lite has been developed based on LPA* and implements the same navigation strategy as D* [83].

3.3 Spatio-Temporal Model for Sensor Cloud Services

We first propose a model for sensor cloud services. Spatio-temporal features will be the focal aspects of this model. The collected sensor data will be analysed and abstracted as sensor cloud services. In this section, we present a formal spatio-temporal model that defines atomic sensor cloud services and service composition. Table 3.1 summarizes the major notations used in the rest of this chapter.

Table 3.1 Summary of notations

Notation	Definition
sen	A sensor
$sen.sa$	The sensing area of sen
$sa.loc$	The center of sa
lS	A line segment sensor cloud service
$lS.p_s$	The start-point of lS
$lS.p_e$	The end-point of lS
$lS.t_s$	The start-time of lS
$lS.t_e$	The end-time of lS
ς	A source point
ξ	A destination point
t_q	A start time of a query
r	A user-defined spatial radius
t	A user-defined time interval

3.3.1 Spatio-Temporal Model for Atomic Sensor Cloud Services

We introduce the notion of a sensor cloud service relying on spatio-temporal aspects. We discuss the key concepts as follows.

Definition 1 Sensor sen. A sensor sen is a tuple of $< sid, loc, sa, tsp >$ where

- sid is a unique sensor ID,
- loc is the latest recorded location of sen,
- sa is the specific sensing area. It is represented as (loc, R_s) in which loc is the center location and R_s is the radius of the area that is covered by sen,
- tsp (timestamp) is the latest time in which sensor data related to a service is collected from sen.

Definition 2 Sensor Cloud Service S. A sensor cloud service S is a tuple of $< id, SEN, space\text{-}time, F, Q >$ where

- id is a unique service ID,
- $SEN = \{sen_i | 1 \leqslant i \leqslant m\}$ represents a finite set of sensors sen_i collecting sensor data related to S,
- $space\text{-}time$ describes the spatio-temporal domain of S. In this chapter, we restrict the $space$ of a service to a $line\ segment$ (called line segment service) that is presented by a tuple $< p_s, p_e >$, where

  - p_s is a GPS start-point of S,
  - p_e is a GPS end-point of S.

  The $time$ is a tuple $< t_s, t_e >$, where

  - t_s is a start-time of S,
  - t_e is an end-time of S.

Fig. 3.2 Line segment sensor
cloud service model

- F describes a set of functions offered by S (e.g., access to data related to a bus travel),
- Q is a tuple $< q_1, q_2, \ldots, q_n >$, where each q_i denotes a QoS property of S including freshness and accuracy.

Definition 3 Spatio-Temporal Service Query SQ. A query SQ is defined as a tuple $< \varsigma, \xi, t_q, r, t >$ where

- ς is a source point,
- ξ is a destination point,
- t_q is the start time of a query,
- r is a user-defined spatial radius,
- t is a user-defined time interval.

Figure 3.2 shows the line segment sensor cloud service model. For example, a bus service S_{65} is a *line segment* sensor cloud service travelling from Stop 4 at 5:10 p.m. (i.e., $S_{65}.p_s = Stop\ 4$ and $S_{65}.t_s = 5{:}10$ p.m.) to Stop 54 (i.e., $S_{65}.p_e = Stop\ 54$ and $S_{65}.t_e = 5{:}22$ p.m.).

A user issues a query SQ to find a line segment service lS such that the start point p_s of the component service is within a spatial circle centered at a source-point with a user-defined radius r. In addition, the start time of the line segment service t_s should be within the time interval t from the start time of query, i.e., $t_s \leqslant t_q + t$. For the sake of simplicity, we only consider two constraints r and t. For example, considering our scenario, the query $<$'A', 'B', 16:10, 300, 10$>$ means that Sarah wants to travel from point 'A' to point 'B' starting at 16:10 (i.e., $t_q = 16{:}10$). Sarah specifies a walk of maximum 300 m (i.e., $r = 300$) and the maximum waiting time to catch the next transport is 10 min (i.e., $t = 10$). For simplicity, the mode of transport is not considered in our definition.

3.3.2   Spatio-Temporal Model for Composite Sensor Cloud Service

In some instances, an atomic sensor cloud service may not fully satisfy a user's query. In this case, a composition of sensor cloud services may be required. A major issue when defining a composite sensor cloud service is whether its component services are spatio-temporally composable. For example, the invocation of a component train service can only occur within 10 min of a component tram service located in a spatial radius of 300 m which has been successfully invoked. In this section, we propose a new *linear* composability model and linear composite

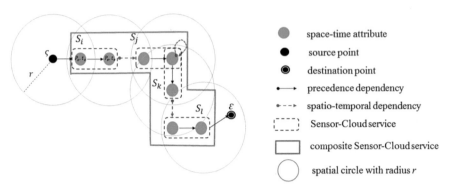

Fig. 3.3 Linear composite sensor cloud service

service. In the remainder of this chapter, the service and composite service are used to refer to a sensor cloud service and composite sensor cloud service, respectively.

3.3.2.1 Linear Spatio-Temporal Composability Model

We define a rule called *linear spatio-temporal composability*. It checks whether two component *line segment* services are spatio-temporally composable with respect to the user-defined maximum spatial radius r and maximum time interval t. In this instance, space and time play the role of non-functional attributes.

Definition 4 (Linear Spatio-Temporal Composability) Two component line segment services lS_k and lS_l are spatio-temporally linear composable if they are both spatially and temporally composable.

- *spatially composable*: Two line segment services lS_k and lS_l are spatially composable if $lS_l.p_s$ is located within the spatial circle centered at $lS_k.p_e$ with a geographic radius r. For example, a bus service 65 using a bus stop 4 is spatially composable with tram service 8 using the tram station 13 (assuming $r = 300$) if there is a walk of less than 300 m between the bus stop and the tram station.
- *temporally composable*: Two line segment services lS_k and lS_l are temporally composable if lS_l will be executed in a time window t of lS_k, i.e., $lS_k.t_e \leq lS_l.t_s + t$. For example, in our scenario, bus service 65 arrives at the bus stop 4 within 10 min ($t = 10$) before departure of tram service 8 from tram stop 13.

Definition 5 (Linear Composite Sensor Cloud Service) LCS. A linear composite sensor cloud service LCS is a sequence of component line segment services $\{lS_i, 1 \leq i \leq n\}$ where each pair of (lS_i, lS_{i+1}) is linear spatio-temporal composable (see Fig. 3.3). Formally, LCS is defined as a tuple $< LCID, LCSEN, LCSPACE\text{-}TIME, LCF, LCQ >$

- $LCID$ = concat $(lS_i.id)$ $1 \leqslant i \leqslant n$ is a concatenation of component line segment services identifiers in which n is the total number of component line segment services,
- $LCSEN = \bigcup_{i=1}^{n} lSi.SEN$,
- $LCSPACE\text{-}TIME$ describes the spatio-temporal footprint of LCS. The $SPACE$ part is defined by a tuple of $< cp_s, cp_e >$, where

  - $cp_s = lS_1.p_s$ in which lS_1 is the first component service of LCS,
  - $cp_e = lS_n.p_e$ in which lS_n is the last component service of LCS.

  and the $TIME$ part of LCS is a tuple of $< ct_s, ct_e >$, where $ct_s = lS_1.t_s$ and $ct_e = lS_n.t_e$.
- $LCF = \{f_1(lS_1), f_2(lS_2), \ldots, f_n(lS_n)\}$, where each f_i is the function provided by the corresponding component services of LCS,
- LCQ is a tuple of $< Q_1, Q_2, \ldots, Q_k >$, where each Q_i is the aggregated value of i_{th} QoS attribute of component services of LCS. For example, the aggregated accuracy value (i.e., Q_1) of a linear composite service is the product of the accuracy QoS of all its component line segment services.

3.4 Spatio-Temporal Selection of Sensor Cloud Services

The service selection problem is to evaluate and select component services so that a composite service provides optimal QoS and meets all QoS constraints. Section 3.4.1 describes how we model the spatio-temporal selection process. In Sects. 3.4.2 and 3.4.3, we present the details of the spatio-temporal indexing model and selection algorithm, respectively.

3.4.1 Spatio-Temporal Candidate Service Search Graph

The QoS-aware spatio-temporal selection problem can be modelled as a directed spatio-temporal graph search problem in which vertices and edges are associated with spatio-temporal attributes and dependencies of services.

Definition 6 A spatio-Temporal Graph $STG =< V, E >$ is a directed graph consisting of a set of vertices V and edges E. Each vertex v has an associated space-time attribute of a service (e.g., (p_s, t_s)) and each edge $((p_s, t_s), (p_e, t_e))$ where $(p_s, t_s), (p_e, t_e) \in V$, $t_s < t_e$ is associated with QoS attributes. If an edge exists, it means there is a precedence or neighbour dependency between two vertices. Neighbour dependency is determined by the linear spatio-temporal composability definition. Figure 3.4 depicts an example of STG in which precedence and neighbour dependency are shown by black solid and red dashed edges, respectively.

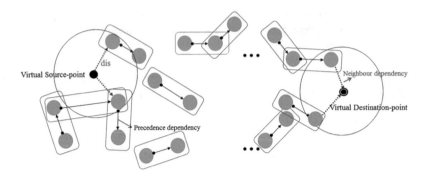

Fig. 3.4 Spatio-temporal graph

A virtual source vertex ς and virtual destination vertex ξ are added to the graph. ς is connected to all neighbour services in radius r and during time interval t considering query initial time t_q. Destination-point ξ is also connected to all neighbour services located in radius r. Since the time at ξ cannot be predetermined, time is not considered in selecting neighbours of ξ. Note that if no service is within the radius r of ς or ξ, the search radius is increased until a service is found.

3.4.2 Spatio-Temporal Index Data Structure for Sensor Cloud Services

There is a need to manage the real-time sensor data exposed as services in the cloud. To address this issue, we index all services. This enables the fast discovery of services. To index services, we should consider spatio-temporal aspects of services. We index *line segment* services by using a 3D R-tree [143]. The 3D R-tree is a spatio-temporal index data structure which efficiently handles range queries of the type "report all objects within a specific area (e.g., a rectangle) during the given time interval" [76]. 3D R-tree adds time as the third axis to spatial axes. Figure 3.5 illustrates how *line segment* services are indexed by a 3D R-tree. The leaf nodes of the 3D R-tree represent start points of actual services which are organized using Minimum Bounding Box MBB that enclose the service spatio-temporal footprint.

Figure 3.6 presents an example of a service query based on a 3D R-tree. A user issues a query about the neighbour services available within a query rectangular region R1 surrounding the source point ς within the radius r. Even though our approach can support any type of spatial shapes, for simplicity, we assume the query region is a rectangular. We compute the MBB to be searched to answer the query. The lower-bound $[x_{min}, y_{min}, t_{min}]$ and upper-bound $[x_{max}, y_{max}, t_{max}]$ of the MBB surrounding $\varsigma = (x, y)$ during the time interval t from a given time t_q, i.e., $[t_q, t_q + t]$ is computed as follows:

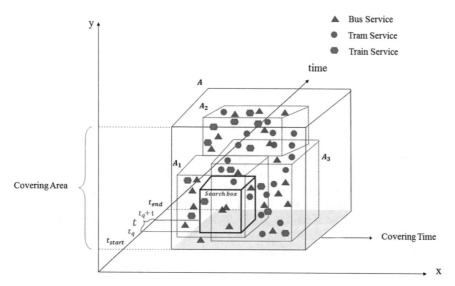

Fig. 3.5 Example of a 3D R-tree for line segment services

Fig. 3.6 Example of a 3D
R-tree query

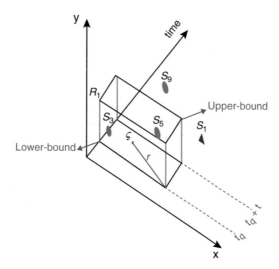

$$
\begin{aligned}
Lower\text{-}bound &= [x - r * cos(45°), y - r * sin(45°), t_q] \\
Upper\text{-}bound &= [x + r * cos(45°), y + r * sin(45°), t_q + t]
\end{aligned}
\tag{3.1}
$$

As a query answer, S_3 and S_5 are two neighbour services expected to be inside
MBB.

3.4.3 Spatio-Temporal Selection Algorithm

To find neighbour services of a given service, we propose a new algorithm *Spatio-TemporalSearch* based on spatio-temporal features of services. We assume that the services are indexed by using a 3D R-tree.

In *Spatio-TemporalSearch*, the minimum bounding box of a service, say *searchbox*, within radius r and time interval t is computed using Eq. 3.1. We then search through the 3D R-tree to find neighbour services which are inside that *searchbox*. For each neighbour, a directed edge is created between the service and the available neighbour service, indicating that a service transition exists (i.e., linear spatio-temporal composability). Moreover, a weight based on the distance between the service and its neighbour service is assigned to the edge for further investigation. For example, every tram service within radius r (e.g., 300 m walk) from a bus stop (i.e., p_e) in the time window 10 min is considered as a neighbour. The time window of 10 min is used to find neighbour tram services which arrive within 10 min from the departure time at the bus stop. Note that there is a different list of neighbours for each query depending on a user's personal preferences with respect to r and t. The details of *Spatio-TemporalSearch* algorithm are presented in Algorithm 1.

3.5 Spatio-Temporal Quality Model for Line Segment Services

Multiple sensor cloud providers may offer similar services at varying quality levels. Given the diversity of service offerings, an important challenge for users is to discover the 'right' service satisfying their requirements. We propose a QoS model that introduces new QoS attributes for line segment services which focus on the dynamic aspects of services. The proposed quality model is also extensible. For the sake of clarity, we use a limited number of QoS. New criteria (either generic or domain-specific) may be added without fundamentally altering the underlying approach.

3.5.1 Quality Model for Atomic Line Segment Services

The proposed quality attributes are as follows.

- *Service time (st):* Given an atomic line segment service lS, the service time $q_{st}(lS)$ measures the expected time in minutes between the start and end points. The value of $q_{st}(lS)$ is computed as follows:

$$q_{st}(lS) = lS.t_e - lS.t_s \qquad (3.2)$$

Algorithm 1 Spatio-TemporalSearch Algorithm

Input: spatio-temporal graph STG, 3D R-tree RT, location loc, start time st, radius r, time interval t

Output: the neighbour list

1: NeighboursList= ∅
2: R = RT → Root
3: searchbox = compute MBB based on loc,r,st,st+t   ▷ Lower bound of searchbox =[loc.x - r*
   $cos(45°)$,loc.y-r*$sin(45°)$, st]   ▷ Upper bound of searchbox [loc.x + r*
   $cos(45°)$,loc.y+r*$sin(45°)$, st + t]
4: **if** R is a leaf node **then**
5:    insert all entries in the R into E
6:    **for** each e ∈ E **do**
7:        flag = true   ▷ To avoid inserting duplicate neighbours
8:        **if** e inside searchbox **then**
9:            **for** each s ∈ NeighboursList **do**
10:                **if** e.id = s.id **then**
11:                    flag = false break
12:                **end if**
13:            **end for**
14:            **if** flag = true **then**
15:                **if** edge(e,loc) ∉ STG **then**
16:                    AddEdge(e.p_s,loc,STG)
17:                    AssignWeight(e.p_s,loc,STG)
18:                **end if**
19:                NeighboursList.insert(e)
20:            **end if**
21:        **end if**
22:    **end for**
23: **else**
24:    insert all entries in the R into E
25:    **for** each child entry c ∈ E **do**
26:        **if** c.MBB overlaps searchbox **then**
27:            Spatio-TemporalSearch(STG,c,loc,st,r,t)
28:        **end if**
29:    **end for**
30: **end if**
31: **return** NeighboursList

- *Freshness (fr):* Freshness indicates the temporal accuracy of a service. Given an atomic line segment service lS, freshness $q_{fr}(lS)$ is computed using the expression $(current\text{-}time - timestamp(lS))$. Since each service consists of a set of sensors $\{sen_1, \ldots, sen_m\}$, $timestamp(lS)$ will be computed as follows:

$$timestamp(lS) = \frac{1}{m} \sum_{i=1}^{m} (current\text{-}time - sen_i.tsp) \qquad (3.3)$$

- *Accuracy (acc):* Accuracy reflects the level of service reliability. For example, a smaller value of accuracy is assumed if fewer sensors contribute to the results of the service. Given an atomic line segment service lS, the accuracy $q_{acc}(lS)$ is the number of operating sensors covering the specific spatial area related to lS. The value of the $q_{acc}(lS)$ is computed as follows:

$$\frac{N_{sen}(lS)}{T_c} \qquad (3.4)$$

where $N_{sen}(lS)$ is the expected number of operating sensors in lS and T_c is the total number of sensors covering the spatial area. $N_{sen}(lS)$ can be estimated based on the number of sen in S, i.e., $|SEN|$. We assume that T_c is known. It is also assumed that all sensors have the same functionalities and accuracy.

3.5.2 Quality Model for Linear Composite Service

The quality criteria defined above are in the context of atomic line segment services. Aggregation functions are used to compute the QoS of composite services. Table 3.2 presents these aggregation functions:

- *Service time:* The service time of a composite service is the sum of the service times of all its component line segment services in addition to the transition time *trans* between two component services. The transition time is computed as follows:

$$trans = \sum_{j=1}^{n-1}(lS_{j+1}.t_s - lS_j.t_e) \qquad (3.5)$$

where lS_j and lS_{j+1} are two subsequent component line segment services and $lS_1.t_e$ is the start time of a query t_q.
- *Freshness:* The freshness value of a composite service is the average of the freshness of all the selected line segment services.
- *Accuracy:* The accuracy value of a composite service is the product of the accuracy of all its component line segment services.

Table 3.2 QoS aggregation functions

QoS attribute	Service time	Freshness	Accuracy
Aggregation function	$\sum_{i=1}^{n} q_{st}(lS_i) + trans$	$\frac{1}{n}\sum_{i=1}^{n} q_{fr}(lS_i)$	$\prod_{i=1}^{n} q_{acc}(lS_i)$

3.6 Spatio-Temporal Linear Composition of Sensor Cloud Services

Given a large number of possible services to explore, a fast algorithm is required to find an optimal composition plan in a reasonable period. We adapt A* algorithm for the spatio-temporal composition. We propose a heuristic algorithm called *LinearComposition* algorithm to find an optimal linear composition plan. The greedy nature of our proposed algorithm ensures that a line segment service chooses a next candidate line segment service that has the lowest cost to the destination among all eligible neighbours. *LinearComposition* algorithm differs from A* algorithm on the *search cost* and *neighbour* functions.

We define *search cost* function *f-score* as follows:

$$f\text{-}score[lS] = g\text{-}score[lS] + h\text{-}score[lS]$$

where *g-score* calculates the cost of selected line segment services from the source-point ς to the current segment location and heuristic function *h-score* estimates the cost from the current point to the destination-point ξ.

Note that *g-score* and *h-score* are normalized before addition in *f-score*. Since the higher value of *g-score* shows the better cost and the lower value of *f-score* and *h-score* present better cost, we use $(1 - g\text{-}score[lS])$.

The *g-score* function is defined as:

$$g\text{-}score[lS] = u\text{-}score[lS]$$

u-score is computed using the following utility function [164].

$$u\text{-}score = \sum_{Q_i \in neg} W_i \frac{Q_i^{max} - Q_i}{Q_i^{max} - Q_i^{min}} + \sum_{Q_i \in pos} W_i \frac{Q_i - Q_i^{min}}{Q_i^{max} - Q_i^{min}} \tag{3.6}$$

where *neg* and *pos* are the sets of negative QoS (e.g., freshness and service time) and positive QoS parameters (e.g., accuracy). In negative (resp. positive) parameters, the higher (resp. the lower) the value, the worse the quality is. W_i, ranging from 0 to 1, is assigned by users to each QoS parameter to reflect the level of importance. Q_i is the *ith* QoS parameter of the composition plan obtained through the aggregate function from Table. 3.2. Q_i^{max} and Q_i^{min} are, respectively, the maximal value and minimal value of the *ith* quality criterion in composite candidates. These two values can be computed by considering candidate services with the highest and lowest values for the *ith* QoS parameter.

Since the performance of the A* algorithm depends on the quality of the heuristics, it is important to use the right heuristics. The proposed heuristic function estimates the cost (i.e., QoS utility score) from the current line segment service to the destination. We assume that the cost of computing the heuristic should not be more than the cost of expanding nodes. As a result, we only consider an estimate of service time.

$$h\text{-}score[lS] = h_{st} \tag{3.7}$$

Our heuristic of service time h_{st} is based on the assumption that selecting a line segment service closer to the destination would find the goal faster. For this purpose, we define h_{st} as:

$$h_{st} = Euclidean\text{-}distance(lS.p_e, \xi) \tag{3.8}$$

i.e., h_{st} estimates the length of the straight line between the end-point of a candidate line segment service lS ($lS.p_e$) and the destination-point. The straight line distance is the shortest distance between any two points based on the triangle inequality theorem. Although a plan based on the straight line plan may not exist, the actual shortest distance is usually close to the straight line distance. Therefore, h_{st} underestimates the cost of service time. To calculate the Euclidean distance, we use the following formula:

$$Euclidean - distance = \sqrt{(\phi_2 - \phi_1)^2 + (\lambda_2 - \lambda_1)^2} \tag{3.9}$$

where ϕ_1 and ϕ_2 are the latitudes of the destination-point and the end-point of lS and λ_1 and λ_2 are the longitudes of the destination-point and the end-point of lS. All latitude and longitude of line segment services are converted to Cartesian coordinates to compute the Euclidean distance.

To find all possible neighbour services (i.e., candidate line segment services) of a service, we define a new *neighbour* function relying on the *Spatio-TemporalSearch* algorithm which searches through the 3D R-tree to find neighbours as discussed earlier. The neighbours are then added to the candidate list. It is to be noted that the QoS attributes of the neighbour edges in the spatio-temporal graph (i.e., spatio-temporal composability as described in Sect. 3.4.1) except service time are set to zero. The service time of the neighbour edge is computed based on the distance between the vertex (i.e., ς or ξ) and its neighbour. For example, in our scenario the service time is computed based on the walking distance between the current service and the neighbour service considering an average walking speed of 4 km/h. The detail of *LinearComposition Algorithm* is presented in Algorithm 2 and Algorithm 3.

Figure 3.7 gives an illustrative example of our approach. At each line segment service, the *LinearComposition* algorithm considers some heuristic-based cost to select the next candidate service with the lowest cost. For example, starting from source-point, there are two candidate services, i.e., lS_9 and lS_{12}. The algorithm selects lS_{12} as the next line segment service to visit based on the search cost $f\text{-}score$. Suppose lS_{12} is visited: from lS_{12} all possible neighbour line segment services are then identified and one of them (i.e., lS_{51}) as another candidate is selected. lS_{12} is then discarded from the candidates. The search cost of existing candidates (i.e., lS_{51} and lS_9) are computed. If lS_9 has the lowest cost, the algorithm backtrack to

---

Algorithm 2 LinearComposition Algorithm

Input: line segment spatio-temporal graph LSTG, line segment 3D R-tree LRT, source-point ς, destination-point ξ, radius r, time interval t, start-time of a query t_q

Output: the optimal linear composition plan from ς to ξ

1:   compositionPlan = $\varnothing$ $\triangleright$ The plan of navigated line segment services.
2:   visitedList= $\varnothing$ $\triangleright$ The list of line segment services already evaluated.
3:   candidateList= Spatio-TemporalSearch(G, LRT, ς, t_q, r, t) $\triangleright$ The list of tentative segment services to be evaluated.
4:   **for** each lS $\in$ candidateList **do**
5:      g-score[lS]= u-score[lS]
6:      h-score[lS]= $h_{st}(lS.p_e, \xi)$
7:      f-score[lS]= g-score[lS] + h-score[lS]
8:   **end for**
9:   **while** candidateList $\notin \varnothing$ **do**
10:      currentS = a segment service in candidateList having the lowest f-score value
11:      **if** currentS.p_e = ξ **then**
12:          **return** reconstruct-plan(compositionPlan, ξ)
13:      **end if**
14:      visitedList.insert(currentS)
15:      candidateList.remove(currentS)
16:      NeighboursList = Spatio-TemporalSearch(G, LRT, currentS.p_e, currentS.t_e, r, t)
17:      **for** each ns $\in$ NeighboursList **do**
18:          **if** ns $\notin$ visitedList **then**
19:             **if** ns.id $\neq$ currentS.id **then**
20:                tentative-g-score   =   g-score[currentS]   +   u-score[ns]+ transitionCost(currentS.p_e, ns.p_s)
21:             **else**
22:                tentative-g-score= g-score[currentS] + u-score[ns]
23:             **end if**
24:             tentative-h-score= $h_{st}(ns.p_e, \xi)$
25:             tentative-f-score= tentative-g-score[ns] + tentative-h-score[ns]
26:          **end if**
27:          **if** ns $\notin$ candidateList or tentative-f-score $\leq$ f-score[ns] **then**
28:             compositionPlan[nsg] = currentS
29:             g-score[ns] = tentative-g-score
30:             f-score[ns] = tentative-f-score
31:             **if** ns $\notin$ candidateList **then**
32:                candidateList.insert(ns)
33:             **end if**
34:          **end if**
35:      **end for**
36:   **end while**
37:   output("No path found! Resubmit your query with relaxed constraints (e.g., waiting time or distance")

---

the previous line segment service and identifies all possible neighbour line segment services (i.e., lS_7) from lS_9. When the end-point of the next line segment service is the destination-point, the search is successful. If the algorithm cannot find a path, a user is asked to resubmit their query with relaxed constraints (e.g., waiting time or distance).

Algorithm 3 reconstruct-plan(compositionPlan, currentS)

1: **if** compositionPlan[currentS] in compositionPlan **then**
2:      p = reconstruct-path(compositionPlan, compositionPlan[currentS])
3:      **return** (p + currentS)
4: **else**
5:      **return** currentS
6: **end if**

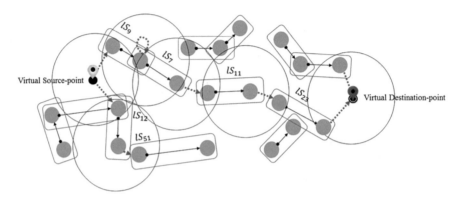

Fig. 3.7 Example of spatio-temporal linear composition algorithm

3.7   Failure-Proof Spatio-Temporal Composition of Sensor Cloud Services

Due to the dynamic environments of sensor cloud, a service may experience significant quality fluctuation at runtime. As a result, an established composition plan may no longer be optimal. We assume that there is a centralized composer system that monitors composite service executions to ensure that the component services are executed successfully. We identified two situations in which an established linear composition may no longer be optimal. First, a component line segment service may provide worse QoS or may no longer be available at runtime and the established composition may fail. Second, the QoS of a component line segment service becomes better and a more optimal linear composition plan may be offered. All linear compositions including the affecting component line segment service should adapt to real-time fluctuation of QoS attributes in such situations. In this section, we propose a novel heuristic failure-proof spatio-temporal service composition algorithm to deal with affecting component services based on D* Lite algorithm [83], called *Failure-proofComposition* algorithm. D* Lite is an incremental heuristic search algorithm which repeatedly determines the shortest path between source and destination points as the edge cost (i.e., QoS cost) of the graph changes. D* Lite is used extensively to solve the goal-directed navigation problem in mobile robot and autonomous vehicle in a changing environment [84].

the *Failure-proofComposition* algorithm is capable of recomputing a new optimal linear composition plan from its current position to destination whenever the overall QoS of the initial linear composition plan significantly changes at runtime. Our proposed approach continually improves its initial linear composition plan and finds the best composition plan from a given source-point to a given destination point while QoS constraints change. We only consider temporal QoS fluctuations in service time Q_{st}. To ascertain the existence of a QoS change at runtime, we measure the value of difference τ between the measured Q_{st} of a line segment service and its promised Q_{st}. If τ is more than a defined threshold ϵ, a Q_{st} change has occurred.

Failure-proofComposition algorithm, like *LinearComposition*, maintains an estimated *g-score* for each line segment service lS in the composition plan. Since *Failure-proofComposition* searches backwards from the destination-point to the source-point, the *g-score* estimates the QoS utility score of the optimal linear plan from lS to the destination. It also maintains a second kind of estimate called *rhs* value, which is one step lookahead of *g-score*. Therefore, it is better informed than *g-score* and computed as follows:

$$rhs(lS) = \begin{cases} 0 & lS.P_e = \xi \\ min_{lS' \in SuccNeighboursList(lS)}(trans(lS', lS) + g\text{-}score(lS')) & lS.P_e \neq \xi \end{cases}$$

$$\tag{3.10}$$

where $trans(lS', lS)$ is the transition time between lS' and lS and *SuccNeighboursList* is the set of *successor* spatio-temporal neighbours of the service lS. The rationale of using neighbours is that the optimal plan from lS to the destination must pass through one of the neighbours of lS. Therefore, if we can identify the optimal plans from any of the neighbours to the destination, we can compute the optimal plan for lS. The successor neighbours of a service lS are identified through the *Spatio-TemporalSearch* algorithm as discussed in Sect. 3.4.2.

By comparing *g-score* and *rhs*, the algorithm identifies all affecting, called inconsistent, component services. A line segment service is called locally consistent iff its *rhs* value is equal to its *g-score* value; otherwise it is called locally inconsistent. A locally inconsistent service falls into two categories: *underconsistent* (if $g\text{-}score(lS) < rhs(lS)$) and *overconsistent* (if $g\text{-}score(lS) > rhs(lS)$). A line segment service is *underconsistent* if its QoS values degrade. In such a situation, the QoS values of affecting line segment services should be updated and the linear composition plan should adapt to the violations. On the other hand, a service is *overconsistent* if its QoS values become better. An overconsistent line segment service implies that a more optimal linear composition plan can be found from the current service. When a line segment service is inconsistent, the algorithm updates all of it's neighbours and itself again. Updating line segment services make them consistent.

Algorithm 4 presents the details of *Failure-proofComposition* algorithm. This algorithm generates an optimal initial linear composition plan like a *backward LinearComposition* search {Lines 33–42}. If the QoS values of component services change after generating the initial composition plan, *Failure-proofComposition*

Algorithm 4 Failure-proofComposition

Input: line segment spatio-temporal graph STG, line segment 3D R-tree RT, source-point ς, destination-point ξ, radius r, time interval t, a set of all line segment services $LSet$
Output: the optimal linear composition plan from ς to ξ

 1: **procedure** CALCULATEKEY(lS)
 2:     return $[min(g\text{-}score(lS), rhs(lS)) + h\text{-}score(lS_{start}, lS), min(g\text{-}score(lS), rhs(lS))]$
 3: **end procedure**
 4: **procedure** UPDATESERVICE(lS)
 5:     **if** $S.P_e \neq \xi$ **then**
 6:         SuccNeighboursList = Spatio-TemporalSearch(STG, RT, lS.p_e, lS.t_e, r, t)
 7:         $rhs(lS) = min_{S' \in SuccNeighboursList}(trans(lS',lS)+ g\text{-}score(lS'))$
 8:     **end if**
 9:     **if** lS $\in$ CandidateQueue **then**
10:         CandidateQueue.remove(lS)
11:     **end if**
12:     **if** g-score(lS) $\neq$ rhs(lS) **then**
13:         CandidateQueue.insert(lS,CalculateKey(lS))
14:     **end if**
15: **end procedure**
16: **procedure** COMPUTEPLAN( )
17:     **while** $min_{lS \in CandidateQueue}(key(lS)) < key(lS_{start})$ or $rhs(lS_{start}) \neq g\text{-}score(lS_{start})$ **do**
18:         CandidateQueue.remove(lS with minimum key)
19:         PredNeighboursList = Spatio-TemporalSearch(STG, RT, lS.p_s, lS.t_s-t, r, t)
20:         **if** g-score(lS) > rhs(lS) **then** g-score(lS) = rhs(lS)
21:             **for all** lS' $\in$ PredNeighboursList **do**
22:                 UpdateService(lS)
23:             **end for**
24:         **else**
25:             g-score(lS) = ∞
26:             **for all** lS' $\in$ PredNeighboursList $\cup$ lS **do**
27:                 UpdateService(lS)
28:             **end for**
29:         **end if**
30:     **end while**
31: **end procedure**
32: **procedure** MAIN( )
33:     CandidateQueue = $\varnothing$
34:     **for all** services lS $\in LSet$ **do**
35:         g-score(lS) = rhs(lS) = ∞
36:     **end for**
37:     $rhs(lS_{destination}) = 0$
38:     CandidateQueue.insert($lS_{destination}$, CalculateKey($lS_{destination}$))
39:     ComputePlan()
40:     **if** g-score(lS_{start}) = ∞ **then**
41:         print "there is no plan"
42:     **end if**
43:     **while** $lS_{start} \neq S_{destination}$ **do**
44:         Runtime monitoring to find the affecting services
45:         **for all** affecting services lS **do**
46:             UpdateService(lS)
47:         **end for**
48:         ComputePlan()
49:     **end while**
50: **end procedure**

---

updates the inconsistent (i.e., affecting) component services and expands the services to recompute a new optimal composition plan {Lines 43–47 }. All inconsistent services are then inserted in a priority queue *CandidateQueue* to be updated and made consistent. *Failure-proofComposition* avoids redundant updates through updating only the inconsistent services which need to be modified, while our *linearComposition* algorithm based on A* updates all the plan. The priority of an inconsistent service in *CandidateQueue* is determined by its *key value* as follows:

$$key(lS) = [k_1(lS), k_2(lS)] = [min(g\text{-}score(lS), rhs(lS)) + h\text{-}score(lS_{start}, lS),$$
$$min(g\text{-}score(lS), rhs(lS))]$$

$$(3.11)$$

The keys are compared in a lexicographical order. The priority of $key(lS) < key(lS')$, iff $k_1(lS) < k_1(lS')$ or $k_1(lS) = k_1(lS')$ and $k_2(lS) < k_2(lS')$. The heuristics in k_1 serves in the same way as $f\text{-}score$ in *LinearComposition*. The algorithm applies this heuristic to ensure that only the line segment services, whether newly overconsistent or newly underconsistent, that are relevant to repairing the current plan are processed. The inconsistent line segment services are selected in order of increasing priority, which implies that the line segment services which are closer to the lS_{start} (i.e., less $h\text{-}score$ value) should be processed first. Note that as the algorithm tracks the execution of the composition plan, the start line segment service lS_{start} becomes the current running service of the plan. Therefore, when a QoS value fluctuates, a new optimal linear composition plan is computed from the original destination to the new start service (i.e., current service). For example, when QoS values increase, the heuristic in the key value ($k1$) ensures that only the newly overconsistent services that could potentially decrease the cost of the start service are processed. When QoS values decrease, it ensures that only the newly under-consistent services that could potentially invalidate the cost of the start state are processed. The algorithm can handle increasing or decreasing the QoS values.

The algorithm finally recomputes a new optimal plan by calling *ComputePlan* function {Line 48}. *ComputePlan* expands the local inconsistent services on *CandidateQueue* and updates the $g\text{-}score$ and rhs values and adds them to or removes them from *CandidateQueue* with their corresponding keys by calling *UpdateService* function {Lines 4–15}. When *ComputePlan* expands an overconsistent service, it sets the $g\text{-}score$ value of the service equals to its rhs value to make it locally consistent {Line 20}. Since rhs values of predecessor neighbours of a service are computed based on the $g\text{-}score$ value of the service (Eq. 3.10), any changes of its $g\text{-}score$ value can effect the local consistency of its predecessor neighbours. As a result, predecessor neighbours {Line 19} of an inconsistent service should be updated {Lines 21–23}. When *ComputePlan* expands an underconsistent service, it sets the $g\text{-}score$ value of the service to infinity to make it either overconsistent or consistent {Line 25}. The predecessor neighbour services of the service need also to be updated {Lines 26–28}. *ComputePlan* expands the services until the key value of the next service to expand is not less than the key value of lS_{start} and lS_{start} is locally consistent {Line 17}.

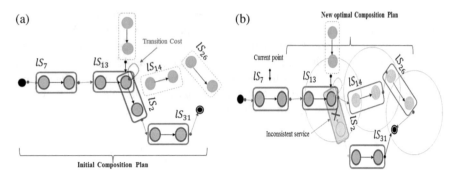

Fig. 3.8 Illustrative example of Failure-proofComposition algorithm. (**a**) Initial optimal linear composition plan. (**b**) New optimal linear composition plan

For example, $LCS = \{lS_7, lS_{13}, lS_2, lS_{31}\}$ is selected as the optimal initial travel plan for Sarah's query (Fig. 3.8a). If lS_2 (e.g., a tram service) is delayed by 15 min (i.e., $\tau = 15$) in its service time, it is highly probable that Sarah will miss lS_{31} (e.g., a bus service). As a result, LCS may fail. In this case, if Sarah is notified of the delay in the middle of the lS_7 journey, she may change her plan. The *Failure-proofComposition* provides a new optimal plan from the current running service lS_7 to the destination. As shown in Fig. 3.8b, the new optimal plan from the current service lS_7 can be $\{lS_{13}, lS_{14}, lS_{26}\}$.

3.8   Performance Study

We conduct several experiments to evaluate the performance of our proposed composition approaches: *LinearComposition* and *Failure-proofComposition*. In Sect. 3.8.1, we discuss our experiment setup. In Sect. 3.8.2, we present the experimental results.

3.8.1   Experiment Setup

To the best of our knowledge, *no* spatio-temporal service test case is publicly available to evaluate our approach. Therefore, we focus on evaluating the proposed approach using synthetic spatio-temporal services. Our evaluation sets a base to which future work will be compared. In our simulation, line segment services are randomly distributed in a 70×70 region. The space and time attributes of services are randomly determined within the range of the region for the simulations. The radius for neighbour search r is set as 5% of the specified region. The remaining service parameters are also randomly generated using a uniform distribution. All experiments are conducted 100 times and the average results are computed. Each experiment starts from different source and destination points which are randomly generated.

The quality parameters of the synthetic line segment services are set as follows. Two QoS attributes are randomly generated with a uniform distribution from the following intervals: $q_{acc} \in [0, 1]$ and $q_{fr} \in [1h, 24h]$. q_{st} is assigned based on the distance between p_s and p_e considering a fixed speed. We assume that service time quality parameter is more important to users. Therefore, the weights provided by users are $W_{st} = 0.6$, $W_{fr} = 0.2$ and $W_{acc} = 0.2$ (Eq. 3.6). The experiments are conducted on a 1.80 GHZ Core i3 processor and 6 GB RAM under Windows 7.

3.8.2 Experimental Results

We perform two sets of experiments. In the first set, we evaluate the performance of linear composition approach in terms of scalability, significance of the heuristic and impact of the radius on optimal plans. The second set of our experiments measures the effectiveness of failure-proof composition approach.

3.8.2.1 Linear Composition Approach

In the first set of the experiments, we evaluate the performance of the *LinearComposition* approach. In these experiments, we show the following. (1) The scalability of our approach over a large number of services and investigate how the execution time varies with the different number of services. We also compare the execution time of LinearComposition with STDijkstra's algorithm which is developed for these experiments. (2) The significance of our heuristic in terms of utility score and (3) the influence of the radius r for neighbour search on the overall utility score value are also shown.

We first compare the execution time of *LinearComposition* algorithm to the execution time of STDijkstra's algorithm. STDijkstra is a special case for LinearComposition when the heuristic is zero, i.e., $h - score = 0$. Figure 3.9 shows the execution time of both algorithms with respect to the density of the graph in terms of the number of services. For this experiment, we keep the default map size, the radius r as 0.5 and time window t as 10 min. We vary the number of services from 2000 to 10,000 with an iteration range of 2000. The results show that the LinearComposition outperforms STDijkstra in terms of execution time (i.e., 21 s $\ll$ 559 s for 10,000 services). It can also be seen that the similar computation time is achieved regardless of the number of services. The slight difference shows the relative stability of our approach.

Next, we study the significance of our heuristic in terms of the overall utility score. We define the optimality ratio as

$$Optimality\ ratio = \frac{v_{stdj} - v_{sta}}{v_{stdj}} \qquad (3.12)$$

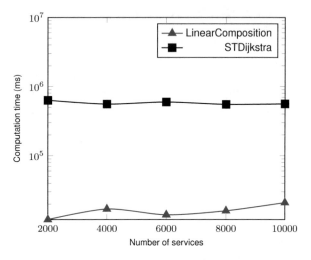

Fig. 3.9 Computation time vs. number of line segment services

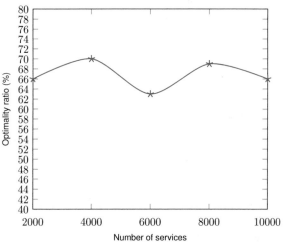

Fig. 3.10 Optimality of LinearComposition algorithm in terms of utility score

where v_{sta} is the utility score of the optimal composition plan given by our heuristic algorithm LinearComposition and v_{stdj} is the utility of the optimal plan given by STDijkstra's algorithm. The utility score shows the cost of component line segment services of the linear composition plan. The higher utility shows better cost in terms of QoS (e.g., freshness, service time and accuracy). We measure optimality ratio while fixing the default map size, the radius r as 0.5 and time window t as 10 min and varying the number of services from 2000 to 10,000 with an iteration range of 2000. Figure 3.10 illustrates that LinearComposition produces a satisfying optimality (i.e., more than 63%). It means that LinearComposition finds more optimal composition plans which may provide better utility. The results also show that the optimality ratio remains quite stable (63–70%) along with the number of services. In general, we can see that the LinearComposition generates more optimal composition plans while the execution time is significantly reduced.

Fig. 3.11 Impact of the parameter r on utility score

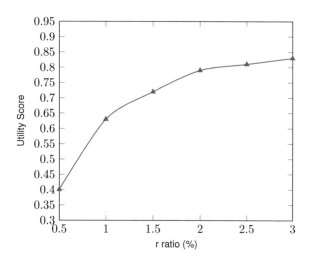

Finally, we assess the impact of the radius r on the overall utility score of a composition plan. The optimal composition plan is the one having the maximal utility score. We maintain the default map size, the number of services as 2000 and time window t as 10 min. We vary the radius r ratio from 0.5 to 3% of the specified map. Figure 3.11 illustrates that the utility score increases by increasing the r ratio. However, there is no significant improvement in the utility score after reaching a threshold (i.e., 1.5). This means that although by increasing the r more neighbours can be found, the time to travel the distance r also increases. Therefore, considering further neighbours cannot significantly improve the utility score.

3.8.2.2 Failure-Proof Composition Approach

The second set of experiments assesses the effectiveness of the *Failure-proofComposition* approach over multiple services and how computation time varies with different QoS fluctuation ratios. We apply the optimized version of D* Lite [83] to implement *Failure-proofComposition*. We test the performance of *Failure-proofComposition* in terms of computation time with the number of services varying from among 100, 1000 and 10,000. For each group of services, we also vary the QoS fluctuation ratio from 5 to 30%. The QoS fluctuation ratio indicates that the ratio of the number of affecting services over the total number of services. For example, a fluctuation ratio of 10% denotes that the service time of 10% of the total number of bus (tram or train) services change at runtime. Figure 3.12 shows *Failure-proofComposition* performs efficiently on a large number of services (i.e., less than 79s to generate an optimal plan on 10,000 services). The computation time increases along with the number of services, which is an expected result. It can be seen that the similar computation time is achieved regardless of the QoS fluctuation ratio. The slight difference (i.e., less than 10 ms over 10,000 services) shows the relative stability of our approach when QoS is highly violated.

Fig. 3.12 Computation time
vs. fluctuation ratio

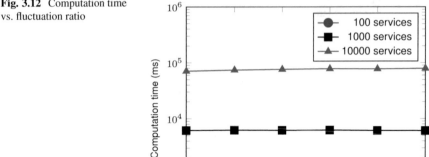

3.9 Chapter Summary

We proposed a novel service framework which integrates sensor data and leverages
novel techniques for the selection and composition of sensor cloud services based
on spatio-temporal features. We introduce a novel spatio-temporal indexing model
based on 3D R-tree to organize and access spatio-temporal sensor cloud services.
In particular, a new quality model is presented that considers dynamic features
of sensors to select and compose sensor cloud services. In addition, an efficient
spatio-temporal linear composition algorithm based on a modified version of A*
is proposed. We also present a novel spatio-temporal failure-proof composition
algorithm based on D* Lite to replan a linear composition plan in case of QoS
changes. The preliminary experiments demonstrate the scalability and performance
of our proposed approaches. The proposed approach may have also some overlap
with other routing contexts such as hand off strategies in ad hoc mesh networks
or social routing [112]. However, the fundamental contribution of this book is the
ability to abstract the problem using the service paradigm focusing on the spatio-
temporal aspects. In future, we plan to implement a prototype and test it with
real-world applications, focusing on building sensor clouds for public transport. We
also plan to compare the performance of the proposed linear approach with other
optimization algorithms (e.g., Krill-Herd algorithm). In addition, we will evaluate
the time complexity of the proposed failure-proof approach under different types of
changes and QoS fluctuations.

Chapter 4
Crowdsourced Coverage as a Service: Two-Level Composition of Sensor Cloud Services

4.1 Introduction

In Chap. 3, we assumed that we have a map consisting of spatial routes which in turn consists of segments. Each segment represents a sensor cloud line segment service (e.g., buses, trams or trains) that has a number of attributes and associated quality of service (QoS). Examples of functional attributes are GPS coordinates and time. The QoS parameters include times of arrival and departure, accuracy and freshness. Therefore, a journey would consist of composing a set of line segment services on the map according to a set of functional and non-functional requirements. We introduce crowdsourced WiFi coverage as a new non-functional and QoS attribute of a line segment service. What we propose in this chapter is to overlay line segment services with crowdsourced WiFi hotspot coverages modelled as region services. This allows users to select the set of line segment services which provide the best crowdsourced WiFi hotspot coverage, i.e., the best quality of experience travelling between two spatial points. The idea is to treat each outsourced hotspot coverage as a service in its own right. The problem of crowdsourced sensor cloud service composition can, therefore, be reformulated as a problem of finding the best set of WiFi hotspot coverages along an optimal linear composition plan using user-defined QoS such as maximum disconnection time and download speed which would be important if the user was watching a movie. Therefore, there is a WiFi hotspot service overlay on the line segment service. It is unlikely that a single line segment service and a WiFi hotspot service would meet a users requirements in a typical geographical plan. As a result, a composition of WiFi hotspot services needs to take place to cover the line segment service. This also means two types of service composition are needed which are correlated, i.e., the linear composition of sensor cloud services to ensure functional requirements and the overlay composition of WiFi services to satisfy WiFi QoS requirements along the travel trajectory.

This chapter focuses on the design and development of a two-level spatio-temporal composition algorithm. In the first level, the overlay service composition

© Springer International Publishing AG, part of Springer Nature 2018
A. Ghari Neiat, A. Bouguettaya, *Crowdsourcing of Sensor Cloud Services*,
https://doi.org/10.1007/978-3-319-91536-4_4

acts as a QoS of the linear service composition that described as Chap. 3. In the second level, we take the first level output as a QoS parameter value to select the best linear composition plan. Functionally, a spatio-temporal overlay composability model is developed to test whether two sensor cloud services are composable using spatio-temporal aspects. We investigate two different approaches for sensor cloud composition. The first approach uses *one segment at a time* to devise the best set of WiFi coverages. The second approach uses *one path at a time* to select the best set of WiFi coverages. We present a set of heuristic algorithms based on the shortest path algorithm like A* and Dijkstra as the basis for finding the optimal linear and overlay composition plan.

The remainder of the chapter is organized as follows. Section 4.2 introduces Coverage as a Service model. Section 4.3 elaborates the details of the double-layered crowdsourced sensor cloud service composition approach. Section 4.4 evaluates the approach and shows the experimental results. Section 4.5 concludes the chapter.

4.1.1 Motivating Scenario

We extend our motivating scenario in Chap. 3 (see Sect. 3.1.1). Here, we assume that Sarah would like to find the best WiFi hotspot-covered travel plan from 'A' to 'B'. As a result, WiFi hotspot coverage is a key QoS parameter to determine the best candidate sensor cloud service. The novelty of this approach is *QoS WiFi hotspot coverage as a service*. Hotspots are complex in nature; they need to be treated as services in their own right. Therefore, we formulate the problem of computing the QoS coverage value as a *composition* of WiFi coverages. Each basic coverage is offered by a hotspot provided by the *crowd*. Consequently, the entire coverage of a journey plan will be *crowdsourced*. For example, Jack may have a high data balance remaining towards the end of the billing period and would like to switch on his WiFi hotspot to share his data balance within a certain period for some cost. Jack can offer a WiFi hotspot service through WiFiMapper[1] or Fon[2] mobile applications. The contexts of participation include multiple variables such as the spatial context (cafe or restaurant), temporal context (duration of hotspot sharing e.g., start-time and end-time) and QoS context (signal strength and bandwidth). Sharing WiFi hotspots can minimize the burden on 3G/4G networks in terms of connections (see Fig. 4.1). We also assume that WiFi hotspots are *static*, i.e., coverage does not change in time and space. The key to crowdsourcing hotspots is the spatio-temporal attributes used for selecting and composing Wi-Fi services. There is an assumption that *no failure* will occur while the user travels along an optimal path.

---

[1]https://www.wifimapper.com.
[2]https://fon.com.

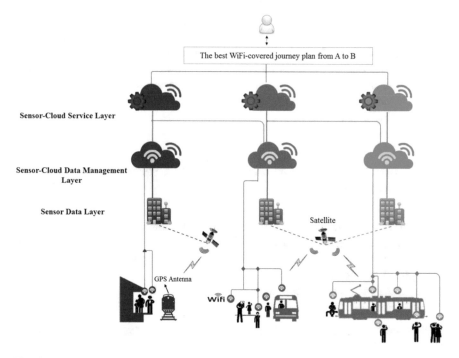

Fig. 4.1 Motivating scenario

This research explores a new area in spatio-temporal travel planning by first abstracting the problem using the service paradigm and then complementing it with the use of crowdsourced WiFi hotspot coverage as a QoS. We take a service-oriented approach to mapping WiFi hotspot sharing as a QoS for planning a service journey. Even more significantly, we consider the coverage QoS as a service itself, reformulating the problem of selecting the best coverage as selecting the best composed hotspot services.

4.2   Coverage as a Service (CaaS)

We model QoS coverage as a service (CaaS). The idea is to treat each coverage (e.g., WiFi hotspot) as a crowdsourced sensor cloud service because of the intrinsic complexity involved in coverage, including area and strength. Therefore, we define this special QoS as a service itself, meaning that it has its own functional and non-functional attributes. In particular, we assume that the coverage with its spatial and temporal aspects represents the functional part. Non-functional attributes include strength, capacity and the level of composability. Given a line segment service, we formulate the coverage QoS as a composition of crowdsourced services (e.g., WiFi coverages) on a line segment service from start-point to end-point. In

Sects. 4.2.1 and 4.2.2, we propose new formal spatio-temporal models for an atomic crowdsourced sensor cloud service and overlay crowdsourced sensor cloud service composition framework, respectively. To select crowdsourced WiFi coverage services, a novel quality model is introduced in Sect. 4.2.3. In the remainder of this chapter, the crowdsourced service and crowdsourced composite service are used to refer to a crowdsourced sensor cloud service and composite crowdsourced sensor cloud service, respectively.

4.2.1 Spatio-Temporal Model for Atomic Crowdsourced Services

We assume that crowdsourced services (e.g., WiFi hotspot services) are typically provided by smartphones. In this research, the smartphones are modelled as sensors to provide real-time information. The WiFi-related data about and generated by the smartphone are stored on the cloud. We introduce a formal crowdsourced service model that abstracts the functionality of crowdsourced data on the cloud in terms of spatio-temporal features as follows.

Definition 7 Atomic Crowdsourced Service rS. A crowdsourced service rS is a tuple of $< id, SEN, space\text{-}time, F, Q >$ where

- id is a unique service ID,
- $SEN = \{sen_i | 1 \leqslant i \leqslant m\}$ represents a finite set of sensors sen_i collecting sensor data related to rS. In this chapter, we assume that each crowdsourced service consists of one sensor or smartphone (i.e., $|SEN| = 1$). Each sensor is represented as (loc, R_s) in which loc is the center location and R_s is the radius of the area that is covered by sen (see Definition 1 in Sect. 3.3.1).
- $space\text{-}time$ describes the spatio-temporal domain of rS. In this chapter, we restrict the $space$ of a service to $region$ (called crowdsourced region service) that is presented by a spatial square area A_s which is a Minimum Bounding Box (MBB) containing the sensing area of rS.

  The $time$ is a tuple $< t_s, t_e >$, where

  - t_s is a start-time of rS,
  - t_e is an end-time of rS.

- F describes a set of functions offered by rS (e.g., providing WiFi hotspot),
- Q is a tuple $< q_1, q_2, \ldots, q_n >$, where each q_i denotes a QoS property of rS including strength and capacity.

Figure 4.2 shows the crowdsourced region service model. It also models, the region service is modelled as an MBB which is represented by (x_s, y_s, t_s) (i.e., bottom-left) and (x_e, y_e, t_e) (i.e., top-right). For example, a WiFi service is a crowdsourced $region$ service that provides WiFi access for a specific area (e.g., bus

Fig. 4.2 Crowdsourced region service model

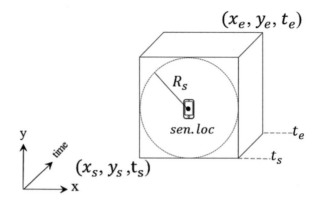

Table 4.1 Summary of notations

Notation	Definition
sen	A sensor
sen.sa	The sensing area of *sen*
sa.loc	The center of *sa*
R_s	The radius of *sa*
R_c	The confident radius of *sa*
rS	A region service
lS	A line segment service
ς	A source point
ξ	A destination point
δ_t	A user-defined disconnection time period
δ_d	A user-defined disconnection distance

station) at a particular time interval (e.g., $t_s = 5$ p.m. and $t_e = 6$ p.m.). Table 4.1 summarizes the key notations used in the rest of this chapter.

4.2.2 Spatio-Temporal Model for Composite Crowdsourced Services

We formulate the problem of determining the QoS coverage as follows: *Given a line segment service (e.g., tram) from p_s to p_e, what is the best coverage (e.g., WiFi hotspot coverage) along the line segment service?* There is a *crowdsourced* service overlaid on the line segment service. It is quite likely that a composition of region services need to take place to cover the line segment service. Therefore, the overlay service composition acts as a *QoS* of the linear service composition. In our scenario, a combination of overlapping WiFi coverages would cover a tram service fulfilling Sarah's requirements which include a maximum disconnection time and distance. To compose crowdsourced services, spatio-temporal dependency constraints between component crowdsourced services are considered. We define a rule called *Overlay spatio-temporal composability*. It checks whether two component crowdsourced region services are spatio-temporally composable. In this case, space and time are highly correlated to the functional part of the crowdsourced service. The existence of a hotspot depends on space and time.

Definition 8 (Overlay Spatio-Temporal Composability) Two component crowdsourced region services rS_k and rS_l are overlay spatio-temporally composable with respect to a line segment service lS iff

- rS_k and rS_l intersect lS and
- rS_l has overlap with the extended MBB of rS_k (i.e., $ExMBB(rS_k)$). The $ExMBB$ (i.e., buffer area) is computed by extending each edge of the area of rS_k by a disconnection distance δ_d and also extending time edge by a disconnection period δ_t (Fig. 4.3). The values of δ_d and δ_t are assumed to be initially defined by the user. For example, Sarah specifies that she may tolerate a maximum of 1 minute's disconnection (i.e., δ_t) in the WiFi connection during the WiFi hotspot handover. We can also determine the disconnection distance δ_d from δ_t considering an average speed.
- Two edge vectors $V_{p_s p_e}$ and $V_{loc_k loc_l}$ are in the same *direction*. The vectors $V_{p_s p_e}$ and $V_{loc_k loc_l}$ connect two vertices (p_s, p_e) and (loc_k, loc_l) respectively. p_s and p_e are the start-point and end-point of lS and loc_k and loc_l are the sensed points of rS_k and rS_l, respectively. The vector direction is used as a heuristic based on the premise that the best neighbours are going to be found in the direction where the traveler is going. The use of path direction also minimizes the number of candidate services in the composition process.

As can be seen in Fig. 4.3, rS_k and rS_l are overlay spatio-temporally composable. However, although rS_m intersects lS, it does not have overlap with $ExMBB(rS_k)$. As a result, rS_m and rS_k are not overlay spatio-temporally composable.

Given a line segment service lS and a set of region services $\{rS_1, rS_2, \ldots, rS_n\}$, we model an overlay composite service as the total union area of component crowdsourced services that cover lS.

Definition 9 (Overlay Composite Sensor Cloud Service) An overlay composite service OCS is a sequence of component region services $\{rS_i, 1 \leqslant i \leqslant n\}$ where each pair of (rS_i, rS_{i+1}) is overlay spatio-temporally composable. Formally, an overlay composite service OCS is defined as a tuple $<$ OCID, OCSEN, OCSPACE-TIME, OCF, OCQ $>$

- OCID = concat $(rS_i.id)$ $1 \leqslant i \leqslant n$ is a concatenation of component region services identifiers in which n is the total number of component region services of OCS,
- OCSEN= $\bigcup_{i=1}^{n} rSi.SEN$,
- OCSPACE-TIME describes the spatio-temporal footprint of OCS. The *SPACE* part is defined by a collection of the total union area of component region services that cover P and the TIME part is a tuple of $< ct_s, ct_e >$, where

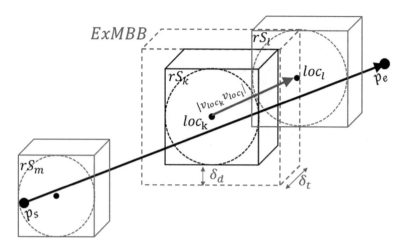

Fig. 4.3 Overlay composite service

- $ct_s = rS_1.t_s,$
- $ct_e = rS_n.t_e.$
- OCF = $\{f_1, f_2, \ldots, f_n\}$, where each f_i is the function provided by the corresponding component region services of OCS,
- OCQ is a tuple of $< Q_1, Q_2, \ldots, Q_k >$, where each Q_i is the aggregated QoS value of i_{th} QoS attribute of OCS.

4.2.3 An Extensible Quality Model for Crowdsourced Region Services

We introduce the QoS attributes for crowdsourced region services. For the sake of simplicity, we use a limited number of QoS attributes. This QoS model can be applied to other applications that involve a sensing region within a particular time.

4.2.3.1 Quality Model for Atomic Crowdsourced Region Services

We propose to use spatio-temporal quality criteria which is part of describing the non-functional aspects of crowdsourced region services:

- *Strength (str):* Signal strength is associated with the sensing area of a region service. The strength depends on the distance between the region service sensed point and the user. For example, in our scenario, the closer the user is to the center of a WiFi service, the stronger is the WiFi signal. We model $q_{str}(rS)$ using an exponential attenuation probabilistic coverage model [11] (Fig. 4.4). In this model, each service has a confident radius R_c. For each region service rS_i,

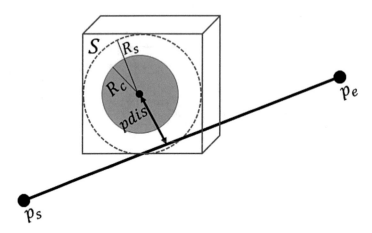

Fig. 4.4 Strength QoS model

$q_{str}(rS_i)$ is computed with respect to the line segment service lS as follows:

$$
\begin{cases}
1 & 0 \leqslant pdis(lS, loc) \leqslant R_c \\
e^{-ka} & pdis(lS, loc) > R_c
\end{cases}
\tag{4.1}
$$

where $a = pdis(lS, loc) - R_c$ and $pdis(lS, loc)$ is the *perpendicular* distance from the sensed point of the region service loc to lS (Fig. 4.4). k is a sensor-technology dependent parameter which varies with the type of sensors and environment. The strength $q_{str}(rS)$ varies from zero to one. Within the distance of R_c, the value of $q_{str}(rS)$ is 1 which means full signal. In the interval $(R_s - R_c)$, the value of $q_{str}(rS)$ exponentially approaches zero as the perpendicular distance increases. Since we assume that a component region service intersects lS, the value of $pdis$ is not beyond R_s (i.e., $q_{str} \neq 0$).

- *Capacity (cap):* Capacity indicates the maximum achievable data rate at which information can be transmitted. It is important for uploading and downloading. Since better signal strength implies higher Signal-to-Noise-Ratio (SNR) (i.e., less error) and therefore more successful transmissions, the user-perceived capacity is directly proportional to the signal strength. We model the capacity based on SNR Shannon-Hartley theorem [130]. We assume that there is a fixed error rate. As a result, the capacity increases as the signal strength increases. Given an atomic region service rS, q_{cap} would be approximately:

$$
q_{cap} = \frac{B}{K} log_2(1 + q_{str}(rS))
\tag{4.2}
$$

where B is the total available bandwidth and K is the maximum number of concurrent requests that rS can support. We assume that total available bandwidth is allocated equally between different users.

Table 4.2 QoS aggregation functions

QoS attribute	Strength	Capacity	Level of composability
Aggregation function	$\prod_{i=1}^{n} q_{str}(rS_i)$	$\sum_{i=1}^{n} q_{cap}(rS_i)$	$\frac{1}{n}\sum_{i=1}^{n} q_{com}(rS_i)$

- *Level of composability (com):* Given an atomic region service rS, the level of composability $q_{com}(rS)$ is the number of available spatio-temporal neighbour region services nS which are located in $ExMBB(rS)$. Since the closer neighbours to the sensing area of rS provide a better composability level, we assign a weight dW based on the distance to rS. q_{com} is computed as follows:

$$q_{com} = \sum_{i=1}^{n} dW(nS_i) \tag{4.3}$$

where n is the number of neighbour services and dW is calculated as follows:

$$dW = \begin{cases} 1 & 0 \leqslant d(rS, nS) \leqslant (R_s + R_{nS}) \\ \frac{1}{(d(rS,nS)+1)^2} & d(rS, nS) > (R_s + R_{nS}) \end{cases} \tag{4.4}$$

where $d(rS, nS)$ is the Euclidean distance between the sensed point of rS and nS. A dW of 1 shows full-composability for the neighbour services that have overlap with the sensing region of rS, while dW is going to zero for the neighbours approaching the borders of the area of $ExMBB$.

Since the range of strength $q_{str}(rS)$ is between 0 and 1, the values of $q_{cap}(rS)$ and $q_{com}(rS)$ are normalized in the range of (0, 1) to overcome the inconsistency between strength, capacity and level of composability. Higher normalized values of $q_{cap}(rS)$ and $q_{com}(rS)$ indicate higher capacity and better composability.

4.2.3.2 Quality Model for Overlay Composite Service

Since a line segment service is covered by a number of region services, it is necessary to calculate the aggregated value of the QoS parameters of those region services. The aggregation functions (Table 4.2) are used to compute the overall QoS value of an overlay composite service as follows:

- *Strength:*
  The strength value of an overlay composite service is the product of the strengths of all its component region services.
- *Capacity:*
  The capacity value for a composite service is the average of the capacities of all its component region services.

- *Level of composability:*
  The level of composability value for a composite service is the average of
  the levels of composability of all its component region services. Note that the
  neighbour services are selected with respect to the given line segment service.

4.3 Double-Layered Crowdsourced Sensor Cloud Service Composition

The process of finding the best WiFi-hotspot-covered journey from A to B is considered as a two-level composition problem. At the first level, the coverage quality
parameter of a line segment service is formulated as the problem of computing an
overlay spatio-temporal composition problem. The second level takes the first level
output as a coverage QoS value of a line segment service to select the optimal linear
plan. A significant aspect is that *the overlay service composition* acts as a QoS of the
line segment service composition. We investigate different approaches to double-
layered crowdsourced sensor cloud service composition. There are fundamentally
two options for computing the best double-layered crowdsourced sensor cloud
service composition. The first option is *one path at a time* to look at the optimal
plans as driven by the linear service composition with the WiFi hotspot services as
the layered composition. The second option is *one segment at a time* to start with the
WiFi hotspot service composition and consider the linear composition as the second
layer of composition. In what follows, we detail both approaches, i.e., *one path at a
time* and *one segment at a time*.

4.3.1 One Path at a Time

At the first level, the *one path at a time* approach applies a variation of *LinearComposition* algorithm as described in Sect. 3.6, returning k optimal linear composition
plans. Given a source point ς and destination point ξ, a linear plan set $\mathbb{P}$ is a set
of k optimal linear plans as shown in Fig. 4.5. The second level takes the first
level output (i.e., $\mathbb{P}$) as an input and applies a new algorithm *FindBestPlan* to

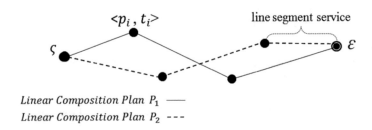

Fig. 4.5 Linear composition plan set $\mathbb{P}$

Algorithm 5 FindBestPlan Algorithm

Input: Linear plan set $\mathbb{P}$, region spatio-temporal graph RSTG, region services 3D R-tree RRT, maximum disconnection distance δ_d, maximum disconnection time period δ_t

Output: The plan with the highest coverage in $\mathbb{P}$ bestPlan

1: max-overlay-u-score=0
2: enclosingMBB = compute the enclosing MBB based on lower-bound and upper-bound

   $\triangleright$ $lower\text{-}bound = [\min\limits_{\forall P \in \mathbb{P} \wedge p_i \in P} P.p_i.x, \min\limits_{\forall P \in \mathbb{P} \wedge p_i \in P} P.p_i.y, \min\limits_{\forall P \in \mathbb{P}} P.t]$

   $\triangleright$ $upper\text{-}bound = [\max\limits_{\forall P \in \mathbb{P} \wedge p_i \in P} P.p_i.x, \max\limits_{\forall P \in \mathbb{P} \wedge p_i \in P} P.p_i.y, \max\limits_{\forall P \in \mathbb{P}} P.t]$

3:   Add all crowdsourced region services inside the enclosing MBB of RRT to a new 3D R-tree NRRT
4: **for** each $P \in \mathbb{P}$ **do**
5:     OCSList = $\varnothing$ $\triangleright$ The list of component line segment services of the optimal overlay composition plan that covers P.
6:     **for** each line segment service IS in P **do**
7:         OCSList.insert(OverlayComposition (RSTG, $IS.t_s$, $IS.p_s$, $IS.t_e$, $IS.p_e$, NRRT, δ_d, δ_t))
         $\triangleright$ OverlayComposition function computes the optimal overlay composition plan that cover IS
8:     **end for**
9:     Compute overlay-u-score[P] based on all component region services in OCSList
10:    **if** overlay-u-score[P] > max-overlay-u-score **then**
11:        max-overlay-u-score = overlay-u-score[P]
12:        bestPlan = P
13:    **end if**
14: **end for**
15: **return** bestPlan

---

determine the best linear plan of $\mathbb{P}$ in terms of WiFi coverage as a key parameter. The idea of our algorithm is to initially prune the search space with respect to $\mathbb{P}$ and select a set of filtered crowdsourced region services over the whole set of candidate crowdsourced region services. A filtering step identifies a spatio-temporal search space which covers all the possible crowdsourced region services that may be involved in the optimal composition plan. We then divide the overlay composition into two phases: *local* for an individual component line segment service of the linear plan and *global* for the whole linear plan. The *local* phase computes the optimal overlay composition plan that covers the given line segment service. The *global* phase combines the optimal overlay composition plans of all its component line segment services obtained from the *local* phase. Finally, the best plan in $\mathbb{P}$ is selected as the optimal solution. Algorithm 5 details the *FindBestPlan* algorithm. In general, this *FindBestPlan* algorithm works in the following four phases.

4.3.1.1   Step 1: Crowdsourced Region Service Filtering

To improve the efficiency of the proposed approach, the first step is to reduce the search space of the algorithm. We develop an MBB that encloses a set of crowdsourced region services relevant to $\mathbb{P}$. The services outside this MBB are assumed to have little probability of being involved in the optimal composition plan. The enclosing MBB is represented by the lower-bound $[x_{min}, y_{min}, t_{min}]$ and upper-bound $[x_{max}, y_{max}, t_{max}]$, where x_{min} (resp. x_{max}) and y_{min} (resp. y_{max}) are the lowest (resp. highest) x-coordinate and y-coordinate among all coordinates of all optimal linear plans. t_{min} and t_{max} are the minimum and maximum time values

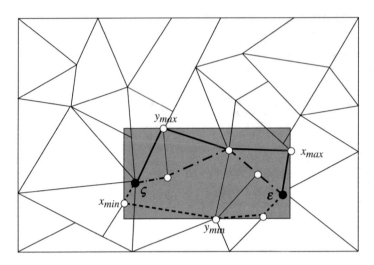

Fig. 4.6 Example of the coordinates of an enclosing MBB

among all time instants of all optimal linear plans (see Fig. 4.6).

$$
\begin{aligned}
Lower\text{-}bound &= [\min_{\forall P \in \mathbb{P} \wedge p_i \in P} P.p_i.x, \ \min_{\forall P \in \mathbb{P} \wedge p_i \in P} P.p_i.y, \ \min_{\forall P \in \mathbb{P}} P.t] \\
Upper\text{-}bound &= [\max_{\forall P \in \mathbb{P} \wedge p_i \in P} P.p_i.x, \ \max_{\forall P \in \mathbb{P} \wedge p_i \in P} P.p_i.y, \ \max_{\forall P \in \mathbb{P}} P.t]
\end{aligned}
\tag{4.5}
$$

3D R-tree retrieves the crowdsourced region services which are inside the enclosing MBB and have overlap with boundaries. All retrieved crowdsourced region services are indexed by a new 3D R-tree, called NRRT (Lines 2–3 in Algorithm 5).

4.3.1.2 Step 2: Decomposition

The decomposition step divides each linear composition plan into elementary line segment services lS which is presented by a line segment of length 1 which consists of two consecutive tuples ($< p_i, t_i >, < p_{i+1}, t_{i+1} >$) (Fig. 4.5).

4.3.1.3 Step 3: Local Spatio-Temporal Overlay Composition

Given a line segment service lS, the local overlay composition step finds an optimal overlay composition plan that covers lS. The spatio-temporal overlay composition problem is modelled as a directed spatio-temporal graph search problem as discussed in Sect. 3.4.1. A virtual start-point vertex ($S.p_s$, $S.t_s$) and virtual end-point vertex ($S.p_e$, $S.t_e$) are added to the graph. The virtual vertices are connected to

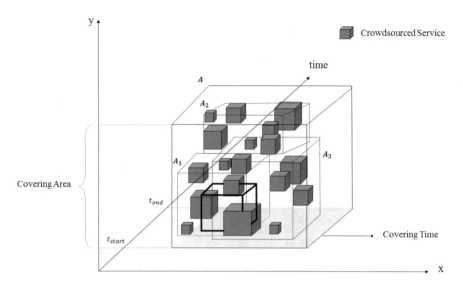

Fig. 4.7 Crowdsourced 3D R-tree

all neighbour region services. The strength, capacity and level of composability of these neighbour services are set to neutral values of one, zero and zero, respectively.

We propose a new algorithm *OverlayComposition* to find the best overlay composition plan that covers the line segment service. *OverlayComposition* is a variation of the Dijkstra shortest path finding algorithm that minimizes the search cost function to find the optimal spatio-temporal overlay composition plan from the start-point to end-point of the line segment service. Our algorithm favours full coverage over partial coverage. *OverlayComposition* differs from the Dijkstra algorithm on the *search cost* and *neighbour* functions. The search cost function of an overlay composition is defined as the following utility function [164] in the same way as the LinearComposition algorithm in Sect. 3.6:

$$u\text{-}score = \sum_{Q_i \in neg} W_i \frac{Q_i^{max} - Q_i}{Q_i^{max} - Q_i^{min}} + \sum_{Q_i \in pos} W_i \frac{Q_i - Q_i^{min}}{Q_i^{max} - Q_i^{min}} \qquad (4.6)$$

We use a spatio-temporal index structure customizing a 3D R-tree for services to efficiently access crowdsourced region services. We assume that the 3D R-tree index of all crowdsourced services are constructed in advance. The leaf nodes of the 3D R-tree represent actual crowdsourced services. Services are presented using *MBB* that enclose the area of a crowdsourced service as shown in Fig. 4.7 (see detailed discussion in Sect. 3.4.2). To find the neighbour region services (i.e., candidate region services) of a service, we define a *neighbour* function relying on the *Spatio-TemporalSearch* algorithm in Sect. 3.4.3 which searches through the crowdsourced 3D R-tree. Keeping all region services in the same direction of the

---

Algorithm 6 OverlayComposition Algorithm

Input: region spatio-temporal graph RSTG, start-time $lS.t_s$, start-point $lS.p_s$, end-time $lS.t_e$, end-point $lS.p_e$, region services 3D R-tree RRT, , maximum disconnection distance δ_d, maximum disconnection time period δ_t

Output: Coverage QoS value

1: compositionPlan = $\varnothing$ ▷ The plan of navigated region services
2: visitedList= $\varnothing$ ▷ The list of region services already evaluated
3:   candidateList = Spatio-TemporalSearch(RSTG, RRT, $lS.p_s$, $lS.t_s$,δ_d, δ_t) $\cap lS$ ▷ The list of tentative neighbour region services which intersects lS and in the same direction with lS
4: **for** each rS $\in$ candidateList **do**
5:     compute u-score[rS]
6: **end for**
7: **while** candidateList $\not\subseteq \varnothing$ **do**
8:     currentS = a region service in candidateList having the lowest (1- u-score) value
9:     **if** currentS.sen.sa.loc = $lS.p_e$ **then**
10:        **return** u-score[currentS]
11:     **end if**
12:     visitedList.insert(currentS)
13:     candidateList.remove(currentS)
14:     NeighboursList = Spatio-TemporalSearch(RSTG, RRT, currentS.sen.sa.loc, currentS.t_e, δ_d, δ_t) $\cap lS$
15:     **for** each nrs $\in$ NeighboursList **do**
16:        **if** nrs $\notin$ visitedList and nrs.id $\neq$ currentS.id **then**
17:          tentative-u-score= u-score[nrs]
18:        **end if**
19:        **if** nrs $\notin$ candidateList or tentative-u-score $\leq$ u-score[nrs] **then**
20:          compositionPlan[nrs] = currentS
21:          u-score[nrs] = tentative-u-score
22:          **if** nrs $\notin$ candidateList **then**
23:            candidateList.insert(nrs)
24:          **end if**
25:        **end if**
26:     **end for**
27: **end while**
28: return 0

---

line segment service using overlay composability model also prevents generating a loop in the search graph.

The details of *OverlayComposition* are shown in Algorithm 6. The input of Algorithm 6 is the space-time attributes of a line segment service lS, a spatio-temporal graph of region services, a 3D R-tree of region services, maximum disconnection distance δ_d and maximum disconnection period δ_t. The output is the coverage QoS value of the given line segment service. The algorithm starts finding neighbour region services of the start-point of lS. The *u-score* of all region services in the candidate list are computed (Lines 4–6). The algorithm selects the candidate region service with the lowest cost as the next candidate to be examined. Given that the higher value of *u-score* indicates better QoS, we use $(1 - u\text{-}score)$. The candidate service with the smallest *u-score* becomes the current service (Line 8). For the current service, all its unvisited neighbours are considered and their tentative *u-scores* are computed (Lines 14–18). If the current service location is the end-point of the line segment service (i.e., the search is successful) (Lines 9–11) or if the candidate list is empty (i.e., the coverage value is zero) (Line 7), the algorithm terminates. Otherwise, the algorithm selects the candidate region service with the smallest tentative *u-score* and, sets it as the new current region service and continues (Lines 19–25).

We proceed now to describe how the spatio-temporal selection of linear composable segment services is performed.

4.3.1.4 Step 4: Global Overlay Composition

After performing the *local overlay* (Line 7, Algorithm 5), each line segment service ends up with an optimal overlay composition plan which covers that service. The *global overlay* step takes the output of all *local overlays*, combines them as an overlay composite service and computes the overlay utility score of the composite crowdsourced service for each linear plan P_i (Line 9, Algorithm 5). The best plan of $\mathbb{P}$ is the linear plan with the highest overlay utility score (i.e., coverage QoS value) of the composition process (Lines 10–13, Algorithm 5).

4.3.2 One Segment at a Time

The *one segment at a time* approach first determines WiFi coverage QoS value along every line segment service using the *overlayComposition* algorithm as the first level composition and then applies a variation of the linear composition algorithm for selecting the best linear composition plan from a source point ς to a destination point ξ as the second level. This approach is more accurate than the previous one (i.e., one path at a time) because it considers coverage as a QoS parameter in addition to the other QoS parameters to select the best candidate line segment service during the linear composition process.

The first level works in the same way as Step 3 in the former approach (in Sect. 4.3.1). Through this level, we determine the coverage QoS values of all crowdsourced region services. In the second level, we only modify the heuristic function of the *linearComposition* algorithm (see Sect. 3.6) to find an optimal linear composition plan considering coverage QoS. It also needs to be noted that the aggregate coverage value of an overlay composite service in search cost function is the average of the coverage of all the component line segment services.

We define a new composite heuristic for the *linearComposition* algorithm based on estimates of service time h_{st} and coverage h_{cov}. Since the value of $h_{st} + h_{cov}$ may be greater than 1, the *h-score* may overestimate the actual cost. As a result, we cannot apply the formula $f\text{-}score = g\text{-}score + h_{st} + h_{cov}$. We define the composite heuristic based on Eq. 4.6 as follows:

$$h\text{-}score[S] = W_{st} \times h_{st} + W_{cov} \times h_{cov} \qquad (4.7)$$

where $W_{st} + W_{cov} < 1$.

The heuristic of service time h_{st} is computed in the same way as *LinearComposition* algorithm which determines the Euclidean distance of the straight line between the end-point of a candidate line segment service IS $(S.p_e)$ and the destination-point.

We consider a novel heuristic h_{cov} which is defined as the coverage of the region services. This is based on the assumption that if the number of region services is high in an area, the probability of finding a more optimal overlay composition plan regarding coverage as a service is high. Since actual region services in an optimal

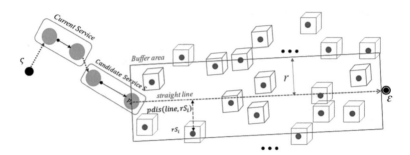

Fig. 4.8 The coverage heuristic

linear composition plan are likely to be close to the straight line, we take into account *proximity* and spatial *distribution* of region services along the straight line. h_{cov} is computed as follows:

$$h_{cov} = \frac{1}{2}(proximity + distribution) \qquad (4.8)$$

To calculate *proximity* and *distribution* values, we first identify the list of region services around the straight line, i.e., $RS = \{rS_1, rS_2, \ldots, rS_{|RS|}\}$. The MBB surrounding the straight line using *Spatio-TemporalSearch* function is computed to find RS. We consider the minimum bounding box MBB of the buffer area of the line. The buffer area of a line is a zone of a specified width around it. Here, we consider a buffer with width r (Fig. 4.8). The time interval of MBB is $[lS.t_e, lS.t_e + maxt]$, where $maxt$ is the time to travel the straight line. The values of *proximity* and *distribution* are normalized before addition.

The *proximity* value measures the number of region services in MBB. Since the closer region service is highly likely to be involved in an optimal overlay composition plan rather than when region services are further from the straight line, we assign a weight based on the distance $pdis$ from the straight line. To assign the weight of *proximity*, for each region service rS_i, the perpendicular distance $pdis$ from the center location of rS_i (i.e., $rS_i.sen.sa.loc$) to the straight line is computed. The value of *proximity* is then calculated as follows:

$$proximity = \sum_{i=1}^{|RS|} \frac{1}{(pdis(line, rS_i) + 1)^2} \qquad (4.9)$$

We propose a method to calculate the *distribution* (variability) of region services along the straight line in the x–y plane. First, the projection of the selected region services (i.e., $rS_i.sen.sa.loc$) onto the straight line is calculated. This eliminates the variability along the orthogonal direction with respect to the straight line as depicted in Fig. 4.9. The constant one is needed to prevent division by zero. We then

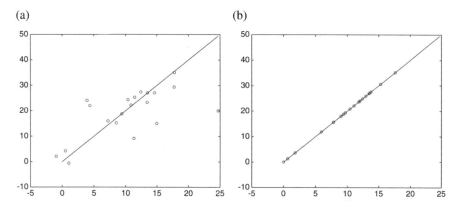

Fig. 4.9 The effect of projection. (**a**) Original. (**b**) Projected

can calculate the variance along the straight line using eigen-decomposition on the covariance matrix of the projected sensed points.

A small variance indicates that the region services tend to be very close to each other, while a high variance shows that the region services are very spread out around the line and from each other.

The mathematical representation of the distribution heuristic is as follows. First, a projection matrix is constructed that projects the crowdsourced region services onto the straight line.

$$\mathbf{P} = \mathbf{r}\mathbf{r}^T,$$

where $\mathbf{r}$ is the vectorial representation of the straight line i.e., $\mathbf{r} = \xi - \mathbf{r}\mathbf{S_j}$. It should be noted that $\mathbf{r}$ is a column vector.

The matrix $\mathbf{S}_{n \times 2}$ represents all the sample region services. Each row in $\mathbf{S}$ represents a region service $r S_i$ in the x–y plane. Therefore, the projected region services can be calculated using the following matrix multiplication.

$$\mathbf{S_p} = \mathbf{SP}.$$

Next, the covariance between columns of $\mathbf{S_p}$ is calculated and the maximum eigenvalue of the resultant covariance matrix is taken as a measure of distribution along the straight line. The eigenvalues of the covariance matrix $\mathbf{C}$ can be calculated by solving the following equation:

$$\det(C - \lambda \mathbf{I}) = 0,$$

where $\det(\cdot)$ is the determinant function and $\mathbf{I}$ is the identity matrix.

4.4 Experimental Results

We conduct a set of experiments to evaluate the performance of both proposed approaches: *one path at a time* and *one segment at a time*. In these experiments, we show (1) the scalability of our approaches over a large number of services and investigate how the execution time varies as the number of services becomes larger, and (2) the significance of our filtering step and heuristic in terms of execution time. We run our experiments on a 3.40 GHZ Intel Core i7 processor and 8 GB RAM under Windows 7. All the algorithms are implemented in Python.

4.4.1 Experiment Setup

To the best of our knowledge, there is *no* usable and relevant real spatio-temporal service (e.g., crowdsourced WiFi hotspot service) test case publicly available to evaluate our approach. Therefore, we focus on evaluating the proposed approach using synthetic spatio-temporal services. Our evaluation sets a baseline against which future work will be compared. In our simulation, line segment and region services are randomly distributed in a 70×70 region. The space and time attributes of services are randomly determined within the range of the region for the simulations. The radius for neighbour search r is set as 5% of the specified region. To obtain a more realistic approach, we use heterogeneous sensors for region services by varying the values of these parameters which are set as follows. R_s and R_c are specified by a ratio of the region size (sensing ratio size) and a ratio of the sensing radius R_s (confident ratio size). The default sensing ratio size and confident ratio size are uniformly selected within a range of $[0.05, 0.1]$ and $[0.4, 0.6]$, respectively. The remaining service parameters are also randomly generated using a uniform distribution. All experiments are conducted 100 times and the average results are computed. Each experiment starts from a different source and destination point which are randomly generated.

The quality parameters of the synthetic line segment services are set as follows. Two QoS attributes are randomly generated with a uniform distribution from the following intervals: $q_{acc} \in [0, 1]$ and $q_{fr} \in [1h, 24h]$. q_{st} is assigned based on the distance between p_s and p_e considering a fixed speed. We assume that coverage and service time quality parameters are more important to users. Therefore, the weights provided by users are $W_{st} = 0.4$, $W_{cov} = 0.4$, $W_{fr} = 0.1$ and $W_{acc} = 0.1$ (Eq. 4.6).

We set the quality parameters of the synthetic region services as follows. The strength value q_{str} is assigned at runtime based on the distance between the region service and the line segment service with respect to R_s and R_c parameters. The capacity q_{cap} is also computed based on q_{str}. The level of composability q_{com} is also assigned at runtime based on the distance between the region service and neighbours that have an overlay with the line segment service. We also assume that the weights are provided by users as $W_{str} = 0.4$, $W_{com} = 0.4$ and $W_{cap} = 0.2$.

Fig. 4.10 Computation time vs. number of region services

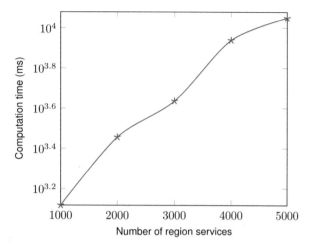

4.4.2 One Path at a Time Approach

In the first set of experiments, we investigate the scalability of *FindtBestPlan* algorithm. For this experiment, we keep the default map size and vary the number of region services from 1000 to 5000 with an iteration range of 1000. Figure 4.10 demonstrates the computation time of our algorithm with respect to the density of the graph in terms of the number of region services. The results show that our algorithm performs efficiently on a large number of region services (e.g., less than 11 s for 5000 services). The computation time increases along with the number of region services, which is an expected result. Note that the computation time shown in Fig. 4.10 does not consider the time to generate optimal linear plans through proposed *LinearComposition* in Chap. 3.

We also study the significance of our filtering stage in terms of the computation time. We define the optimality ratio as follows:

$$Optimality\ ratio = \frac{ct_{wf} - ct_f}{ct_{wf}} \qquad (4.10)$$

where ct_{wf} is the execution time of our algorithm *FindtBestPlan* without filtering and ct_f is the execution time of *FindtBestPlan* by applying filtering stage. We measure the optimality ratio while fixing the default map size and varying the number of region services from 1000 to 5000 with an iteration range of 1000. Figure 4.11 illustrates that the filtering phase produces a satisfying optimality (i.e., more than 83%). This means that applying a filtering stage significantly reduces the computation time which confirms our expectation about its impact on the computation time. The results also show that the optimality ratio remains quite stable along with the number of region services.

Fig. 4.11 Optimality in terms of computation time

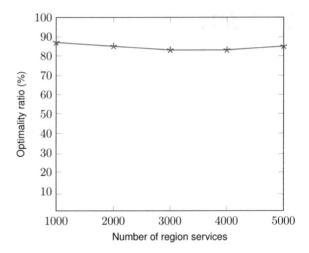

Fig. 4.12 Execution time vs. number of line segment services

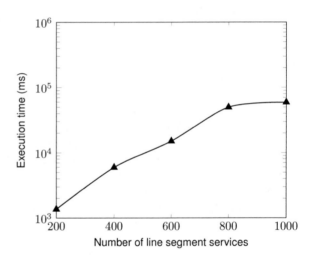

4.4.3 One Segment at a Time Approach

In the second set of experiments, we first investigate the scalability of our modified *LinearComposition* and *OverlayComposition* algorithms. We focus on how computation time varies with the number of both line segment and region services. In the first experiment, we vary the number of line segment services from 200 to 1000 with an iteration range of 200 while the values of other parameters are kept constant. In addition, we uniformly distribute the region services along each group of line segment services. Figure 4.12 shows the execution time of the *LinearComposition* algorithm with respect to the density of the graph in terms of the number of line segment services. The results show that the execution time of

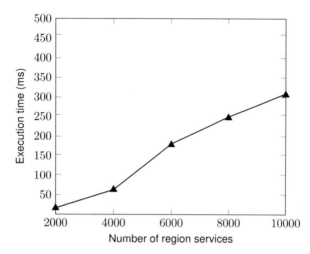

Fig. 4.13 Execution time vs. number of region services

our algorithm increases along with the number of line segment services which is an expected result. This exponential time complexity is basically due to the need to compute a large number of time-consuming shortest path operations to determine the coverage value as the number of line segment services increasing.

We also study the scalability of *OverlayComposition* in terms of the execution time. We fix the number of line segment services to 400 and vary the number of region services from 2000 to 10,000 with an iteration range of 2000. Figure 4.13 illustrates the execution time of *OverlayComposition* algorithm increases by increasing the number of region services because the cost of finding neighbours is significant. The results show that *OverlayComposition* can scale up to 10,000 region services in less than 310 ms.

We study the significance of our heuristic in terms of execution time. We define the optimality ratio as follows:

$$Optimality\ ratio = \frac{\upsilon_{wh} - \upsilon_h}{\upsilon_{wh}} \tag{4.11}$$

where υ_h is the execution time of the optimal linear composition plan given by our heuristic algorithm *linearComposition* and υ_{wh} is the execution time of the optimal plan given by *linearComposition* algorithm without applying heuristic (i.e., *h-score* $= 0$). We then compute the accuracy of the results of our approach by comparing the overall utility value (U_h) of the optimal plan given by our heuristic algorithm *linearComposition* to the overall utility value (U_{wh}) of the optimal plan obtained by *linearComposition* algorithm without applying heuristic. The accuracy is computed by $\frac{U_h}{U_{wh}}$.

We measure optimality and accuracy ratio while keeping constant all parameters and varying the number of services from 200 to 1000 with an iteration range of 200. Figure 4.14 shows that *linearComposition* produces a satisfying optimality

Fig. 4.14 Optimality and accuracy

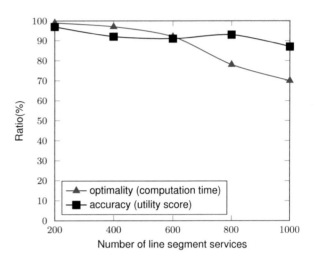

in terms of execution time (i.e., more than 70% for 1000 segment services). It means that applying heuristic significantly reduces the execution time dramatically, which confirms our expectation about its impact on time. Figure 4.14 also shows that *linearComposition* finds almost the near optimal plans with respect to the utility score. The results also show that the accuracy ratio reduces slightly along with the number of line segment services. The slight difference (i.e., less than 10%) shows the relative stability of our approach. In general, we can see that the *linearComposition* generates quite the same optimal composition plans while the execution time is significantly reduced.

4.5 Chapter Summary

We proposed a novel service framework which integrates crowdsourced sensor data and cloud. We also leveraged novel techniques for the selection and composition of crowdsourced sensor cloud services based on spatio-temporal features. We introduced a two-level spatio-temporal composition algorithm to efficiently select the optimal composition plan considering multiple QoS criteria. Even more significantly, we considered the coverage QoS as a service itself, reformulating the problem of computing the coverage value as an overlay service composition. We conducted preliminary experiments to demonstrate the scalability and performance of our proposed algorithms. The results show that our algorithms have a satisfying efficiency in terms of optimality and execution time. The analysis and experimentation presented in this chapter can be extended to consider other possible application scenarios including ride sharing, carpooling and drone sky path planning.

Chapter 5
Incentive-Based Crowdsourcing of Hotspot Services

5.1 Introduction

The success of the proposed crowdsourced service framework in Chap. 4 depends on the willingness of the crowd to participate and offer services. Therefore, it is paramount to consider the incentives as the driving mechanism to increase participation. The context of participation includes parameters such as the *spatio-temporal* context (location and time) and *QoS* context (WiFi coverage). We use a *credit* compensation model for owners of crowdsourced services to encourage greater participations. A crowdsourced service provider will receive credit for the services it provides. Since we assume that crowdsourced service providers may also be service consumers, accumulated credits could also be used when crowdsourcing services from others.

The initial distribution of crowdsourced services may not be an ideal distribution. Some areas might be oversupplied or undersupplied. An area is considered to be undersupplied if the number of supplied crowdsourced service providers are less than the number of demanded service providers (i.e., potential users) and vice versa. Therefore, the redistribution of crowdsourced services is required to achieve better balanced coverage in each area. As a result, there is a need for an incentive model to move a certain proportion of sensor cloud service providers from oversupplied regions to undersupplied regions to fulfil various environment-based coverage demands. This movement also helps crowdsourced service providers to earn more credits. In this chapter, we propose a new spatio-temporal incentive model which creates different incentives for different areas. The differences among incentives depend on the dynamic spatio-temporal sensor cloud environment. In this regard, we consider the spatio-temporal density and location entropy in designing the incentive model. Therefore, service providers are incentivized according to the area's demands.

The major contribution of this chapter is a novel redistribution algorithm that offers incentives to crowdsourced service providers to achieve an optimal balanced

© Springer International Publishing AG, part of Springer Nature 2018
A. Ghari Neiat, A. Bouguettaya, *Crowdsourcing of Sensor Cloud Services*,
https://doi.org/10.1007/978-3-319-91536-4_5

coverage. In the algorithm, we try to reach coverage equilibrium in an iterative process where crowdsourced service providers in the oversupplied areas move to undersupplied areas. The proposed approach is based on a novel participation probability model that estimates the expected number of crowdsourced service providers in the redistribution process. We focus on the use of WiFi hotspot sharing in a geographical area. Finally, we present the performance study of the proposed approach in terms of both its effectiveness and scalability using real-world datasets. The proposal aims to provide users with the best Quality of Experience (QoE) along a WiFi-covered travel plan by redistributing hotspot coverage in a predefined geographic region.

This chapter is organized as follows. Section 5.2 illustrates the related work. Section 5.3 provides an overview of the system model and defines the problem. Section 5.4 elaborates the details of the proposed spatio-temporal incentive-based approach. Section 5.5 evaluates the approach and shows the experimental results. Section 5.6 concludes the chapter.

5.1.1   Motivating Scenario

The problem of crowdsourced service coverage is illustrated using the real-world scenario of WiFi hotspot sharing as in Chap. 4. We assume that WiFi hotspot services are typically provided by smartphones. We consider smartphones as sensors that provide real-time information which is stored in the cloud. In this context, we model the WiFi hotspot coverage as a service. We assume that WiFi hotspot coverage information will be overlaid on digital maps. It allows users to select the set of road segments which provide the best WiFi hotspot coverage, i.e., the best quality of experience when travelling between two spatial points. Each basic coverage is offered by the crowd as hotspot providers (see Fig. 5.1).

We assume that there is a virtual credit system which incentivizes the crowd participation. Users of hotspots may use credits to purchase premium services from hotspot services. Hotspot providers earn credits by participating in this space.

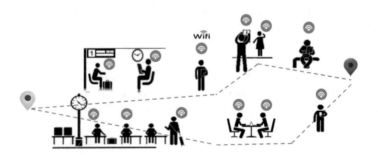

Fig. 5.1 WiFi hotspot sharing scenario

Similarly, users of WiFi hotspots pay in credits for consuming hotspot services. The problem of crowdsourced service coverage can be reformulated as *providing an optimal demanded coverage of crowdsourced services along the route using incentives to provide users with the best QoE.*

5.2 Background

There have been several pricing modules and rewarding mechanisms in crowdsourcing systems as discussed in Sect. 2.4. Incentives act as a powerful tool to change habits. For example, in the Netherlands, users are rewarded to change their travel behavior during the morning rush-hour through switching to another travel mode or changing their schedules [18]. During periods of excessive demand, the ride-sharing company Uber also applies a surge pricing algorithm to temporarily increase normal fares for a particular geographic location at particular time to encourage drivers to flood undersupplied regions [33]. We take slightly different approach that tries to reach equilibrium in an iterative process by rewarding hotspot providers to move from only oversupplied regions to assigned undersupplied regions.

Our work is also related to an online spatial task assignment problem in mobile crowdsourcing due to the assignment of crowdsourced service providers to achieve coverage balancing and the spatio-temporal nature of crowdsourced services. [62] and [63] present frameworks for online task assignments in which heterogeneous tasks must be assigned to workers. [60] studies the problem of task allocation for spatial crowdsourcing applications with the key objective of maximizing the reward taking into account a time constraint for each worker. They also propose an efficient pricing mechanism in which each mobile user reaches an agreement on the price of each task. [80] proposes the task assignment problem in spatial crowdsourcing with the aim of maximizing the number of performed tasks per worker. This work is extended in [145] to a maximum score assignment problem. Two greedy offline and online task assignment algorithms that minimize the average makespan of all tasks are also proposed in [156]. [37] presents a unified framework for task matching and task scheduling based on flow network. Our aim is different from the aforementioned studies; it is to achieve a demanded coverage of crowdsourced services. The strength of the proposed framework is also the ability to combine techniques from incentive models and task assignment in spatio-temporal crowdsourcing systems.

5.3 System Model and Problem Formulation

This section presents a formal model for our spatio-temporal crowdsourced coverage balance problem. We consider the scenario of crowdsourced WiFi hotspot sharing in a selected spatial region during a particular time interval τ. The system consists of a central server that is assumed to be fully aware of the crowdsourced services' distribution. We use the following definitions to formulate the problem.

Definition 10 (Crowdsourced Service) In Chap. 4, we defined a crowdsourced service S with a center location (i.e., longitude and latitude) and the radius of the sensing region, start-time t_s, end-time t_e, a set of functions offered by S (e.g., providing a WiFi hotspot) and a set of QoS attributes q_i (e.g., strength, capacity and level of composability).

Definition 11 (Crowdsourced Service Provider) A crowdsourced service provider as described in Chap. 4 and denoted by sp, is a person who volunteers to provide crowdsourced service through their smartphone. We assume that crowdsourced service providers may also be crowdsourced service consumers.

Definition 12 (Region and Subregion) The server divides the entire region into a set of subregions $SR = \{sr_1, sr_2, \ldots\}$ (of different sizes according to the system's service granularity requirement). For example, each suburb (i.e. zip code) in the city of San Francisco (i.e. region) is defined as a subregion. Each subregion is composed of a coordinator, a set of crowdsourced service providers $SP = \{sp_1, sp_2, \ldots\}$ and a set of potential users who are willing to access the Internet through WiFi hotspot of sp_i. A subregion coordinator is the system that monitors the shortage of the subregion to ensure that the demanded services are provided.

The server also divides the entire time interval τ into a set of discrete time slots, denoted as $\{t_1, t_2, t_3, \ldots\}$ based on the maximum travel time between two subregions using Google Map Distance Matrix API.[1] Within each subregion and within a certain time slot, a certain number of crowdsourced service providers are required: this is set by the coordinator as demand. As a result, each subregion sr_i maintains the number of supplied hotspot providers (i.e., supply) N_s and the number of demanded hotspot providers (i.e., demand or potential users) N_d. We now define the notions of *oversupplied* and *undersupplied* subregions.

Definition 13 (Undersupplied and Oversupplied Subregion) In the time slot t_i, given supply N_s and demand N_d of a subregion sr_i, sr_i is said to be undersupplied if $N_d > N_s$. If $N_d < N_s$, sr_i is said to be oversupplied.

Definition 14 (Balanced Subregion) A subregion is balanced if $N_d = N_s$.

In our model, we take into consideration a credit compensation approach to incentivize the crowd to offer their data as a service. We formally define the notion of an incentive as follows.

Definition 15 (Incentive) The crowdsourced service provider receives an *incentive* (i.e., reward) by participating. Each incentive is earned as credit points that can be stored. We assume that at the outset an initial budget is assigned to all users. It is the same for all users to ensure fairness.

---

[1]https://developers.google.com/maps/documentation/distance-matrix/intro.

Definition 16 (Incentive Advertisement) In each time slot t_i, the coordinator of the undersupplied subregion sr_i advertises an incentive to encourage crowdsourced service providers to move from oversupplied subregions to sr_i. The coordinator specifies its incentive value based on several spatio-temporal factors including density, time of day and subregion entropy. The crowdsourced providers in oversupplied subregions will also decide to move based on several parameters including the advertised incentive. Therefore, the higher incentive in some undersupplied subregions can motivate more crowdsourced providers to move into undersupplied suregions.

Definition 17 (Region Coverage Equilibrium) Given a set of subregions $\{sr_1, sr_2, \ldots\}$ and their corresponding supplies N_s and demands N_d, a region is in coverage equilibrium if and only if :

$$for\ all\ sr_i \in SR, \ \frac{sr_i.N_d}{sr_i.N_s} \leq 1 \tag{5.1}$$

Based on above definitions, we now formally define the problem of crowdsourced coverage balancing with incentive.

Definition 18 (Crowdsourced Coverage Balance Problem) Given a time interval $\tau = \{t_1, t_2, t_3, \ldots\}$ and a set of subregions $\{sr_1, sr_2, \ldots\}$, let $SP_{ij} = \{sp_1, sp_2, \ldots\}$ be the set of hotspot providers in the time slot t_i in the subregion sr_j. The crowdsourced coverage balance problem is to redistribute service providers within subregions during the time interval τ through offering incentives, while achieving coverage equilibrium.

Figure 5.2 shows the proposed system architecture. The undersupplied subregions coordinators advertise their desired incentive to the server in the time slot t_i (Step 1). Next, the server disseminates the incentive offers to all crowdsourced providers of oversupplied subregions (Step 2). Then, the server computes the participation probability of a crowdsourced hotspot provider to move to undersupplied subregions sr_i and sr_j. This is determined based on several probability values each of which reflects the provider's willingness to response positively to an incentive offer (e.g. the probability value that an oversupplied provider participates and moves to sr_i based on the distance is 60%) (Step 3). Thereafter, the server assigns the providers of oversupplied subregions to move to undersupplied subregions based on their participation probability (Step 4). The server then sends the movement request to providers of oversupplied subregions (Step 5). Upon receiving the request, a provider decides whether to move or not. If yes, it sends a consent message to the server confirming its movement (Step 6). If a provider is not willing to move, no consent message is sent. We use the following assumptions in our system model:

- Each subregion has *autonomous incentive* advertisements. In the system, subregions advertise incentives based on their own model. They are autonomous while determining their own desired incentive values.

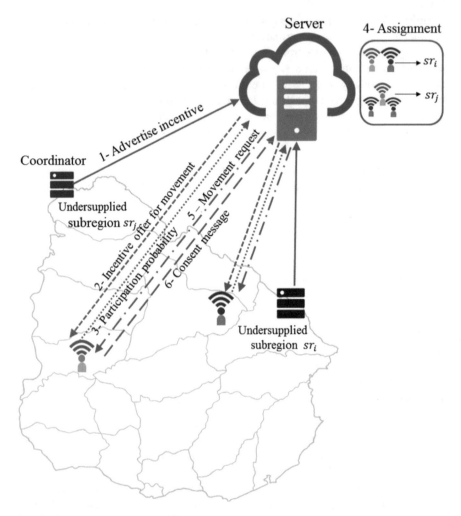

Fig. 5.2 The proposed system architecture

- We only consider *transition* of crowdsourced service providers from oversupplied subregions to undersupplied subregions.
- The total number of crowdsourced service providers and consumers are static over time.
- We assume that each hotspot provider from oversupplied subregions is assigned to each demanded hotspot provider.

The major notations used in the rest of the chapter are summarized in Table 5.1. In the remainder of this chapter, the terms *hotspot service* and *hotspot provider* refer to a crowdsourced service and crowdsourced service provider respectively.

Table 5.1 Summary of notations

Notation	Definition
sp	A crowdsourced service provider
SP	Set of crowdsourced service providers
sr	A subregion
SR	Set of subregions that partition the whole area
τ	Time interval under consideration
t_i	A time slot
osr	Oversupplied subregion
usr	Undersupplied subregion
M	The transition matrix
P	The participation probability
ε	The equilibrium ratio
N_s	Number of supplied crowdsourced service providers
N_d	Number of demanded crowdsourced service providers
G	Bipartite graph
osv	Oversupplied subregion vertex
usv	Undersupplied subregion vertex
C	Capacity of a vertex
f	Flow of an edge

5.4 Spatio-Temporal Incentive-Based Approach

In this section, we propose a novel spatio-temporal incentive-based approach to encourage movement from oversupplied subregions to undersupplied subregions. This movement helps crowdsourced hotspot providers to earn more incentives. Distributing crowdsourced services may help to achieve a better balanced crowdsourced coverage among the subregions. In Sect. 5.4.1, we define the coverage equilibrium. Then Sects. 5.4.3 and 5.4.2 detail the proposed incentive model and participation probability model respectively. Finally, we present our novel greedy approach to redistribute hotspot providers in Sect. 5.4.4.

5.4.1 Coverage Equilibrium of Hotspot Providers

Each subregion sr_i in the map maintains the number of supplied hotspot providers (i.e., supply) N_s and the number of demanded hotspot providers (i.e., demand or potential users) N_d. These values are updated at the beginning of each time slot t_i. The aim of our model is to continuously update supply and demand values to achieve a balanced coverage among subregions during the time interval τ. The interval is divided into a set of equal fixed length time slots which is computed based on maximum travel time between two subregions of the region. Therefore, within

Fig. 5.3 The number of
hotspot providers among each
subregion histogram in the
time slot t_i

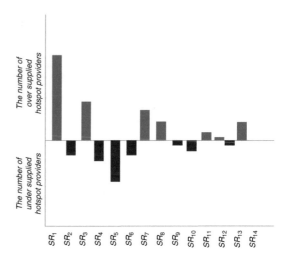

the time slot, each hotspot provider is able to move to the assigned subregion. We
use the difference of N_s and N_d to determine the surplus or shortage of providers in
a subregion. Figure 5.3 shows an example of the histogram of the initial distribution
of hotspot providers in each subregion in the time slot t_i. The initial (surplus or
shortage) distributions of the hotspot providers (without incentives) may not be
the ideal distribution. For example, in Fig. 5.3 the coordinator of the subregion sr_2
may require at least 50 hotspot providers to meet its demand. However, sr_2 has 22
providers which are fewer than 50 hotspot providers. As a result, some subregions
can be undersupplied (e.g., sr_2) while others are oversupplied (e.g., sr_1).

Therefore, we require redistribution of some hotspot providers to reach coverage
equilibrium. The region coverage equilibrium occurs at the point at which the ratio
of the number of hotspot providers supplied and the number of hotspot providers
demanded for each subregion is less than one. Given a set of subregions $sr =
\{sr_1, sr_2, \ldots\}$, the equilibrium ratio ε is computed as the ratio between the sum of
the number of supplied hotspot providers and the sum of the number of demanded
hotspot providers among all subregions as follows:

$$\varepsilon = \frac{\sum_{i=1}^{n} sr_i.N_s}{\sum_{i=1}^{n} sr_i.N_d} \qquad (5.2)$$

We recompute the surplus and shortage of providers in each subregion using the
computed equilibrium ratio as follows:

$$\delta_{sr_i} = \lfloor sr_i.N_s - (sr_i.N_d \times \varepsilon) \rfloor \qquad (5.3)$$

Our goal is to reach a coverage equilibrium during the time interval τ.

5.4.2 *Incentive Model*

The crowdsourced hotspot supply among some subregions e.g., sr_1 and sr_3 is significantly higher than the supply in subregions sr_2 and sr_9. The higher incentive values in some subregions may motivate hotspot providers in the oversupplied subregions (e.g., sr_1 and sr_3) to move into an undersupplied subregion (e.g., sr_2) and provide the hotspot service. The motivations can be categorized as intrinsic or extrinsic [126]. Intrinsic motivation occurs when an individual engages in an activity because of its inherent satisfactions generated by the activity such as interest or enjoyment. Extrinsic motivation is doing an activity to achieve a certain desired outcome such as material incentives [36]. Rewarding can also be further divided into tangible (monetary) and intangible (non-monetary) (also called recognition). Tangible rewards can be demonstrable and measurable such as money and awards. Intangible rewarding is internal and psychological (e.g., giving membership privileges and public recognition) [12]. Since the WiFi hotspot sharing is a simple task and do not demand creativity, it can be assumed that a key incentive to participate is intrinsic motivation through achieving a tangible reward such as credit.

The coordinator of an undersupplied subregion sets its desired incentive value (called reward) to transfer providers among subregions. Several factors including subregion density, subregion entropy and time of day affect the reward value, which changes over time. To compute the reward value, we consider the following spatio-temporal features:

- Subregion entropy
  We consider the *popularity* of a subregion to determine the reward. This is calculated using *Location Entropy*. *Location Entropy* was first introduced in [34] to measure the diversity of *unique* visitors to a region. We use entropy of a subregion to measure the total number of hotspot providers in that subregion as well as the relative proportion of their future service provisioning (or visits) in that subregion. A subregion has a high entropy if many hotspot providers offer services in that subregion in equal proportion of services. Conversely, a subregion has a low entropy if the distribution of the hotspot providers to that subregion is restricted to only a few hotspot providers. Intuitively, higher reward is offered to provider to move to subregions with smaller location entropy (i.e., less popular), because those subregions are less likely to be serviced by other hotspot providers. For a subregion sr_i, let $SP_{sr_i} = \{sp \in SP : sp\ offers\ a\ hotspot\ service\ in\ sr_i\}$ be the set of all *unique* hotspot providers who offer services in sr_i. Let S_{sr_i} be the set of all services offered by all hotspot providers in sr_i and S_{sr_i,sp_k} be the set of services in sr_i that are offered by sp_k. The probability that a random draw from S_{sr_i} belongs to S_{sr_i,sp_k} is $P_{sr_i}(sp_k) = \frac{S_{sr_i,sp_k}}{S_{sr_i}}$ which is the total fraction of all services in sr_i that are offered by the hotspot service provider sp_k. The subregion entropy of sr_i is computed as follows:

$$SRE_i = - \sum_{sp_k \in SP_{sr_i}} P_{sr_i}(sp_k) \times log\,P_{sr_i}(sp_k) \qquad (5.4)$$

Fig. 5.4 An example of
subregion entropy (SRE)

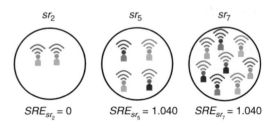

The reward value decreases when the entropy is higher in a particular subregion, because hotspot service provisioning is highly probable in future, even if the frequency of the hotspot providers in the subregion is low. Figure 5.4 shows an example of subregion entropy for three hotspot providers. The subregion entropy is not calculated based on the total number of hotspot services. However, it is determined based on the number of services that offered by unique hotspot providers (e.g., sr_5 and sr_7 have the same entropy i.e., 1.040 regardless of different total number of four and eight services, respectively). As a result, our model assigns higher reward to encourage the crowd to move to less popular areas.

- Spatio-temporal density

  The reward is increased if there is an excessive demand in a particular subregion. The reward is determined based on the difference between the levels of supply and demand. For example, since there is more demand than supply during peak hours, the coordinator sets higher reward to incentivize more hotspot providers. In this regard, we take into account the spatio-temporal density of hotspot providers as one of the parameters to calculate the reward. Our model assigns a higher reward to encourage the crowd to move to sparse areas. The density is computed as the total number of demanded hotspot providers N_d in sr_i in the time slot t_i divided by the total number of supplied hotspot providers N_s in sr_i in the time slot t_i, $D_{t_i}(sr_i) = \frac{N_d}{N_s}$.

- Time of day

  Time is an important parameter in determining the reward. For example, the reward of providing a hotspot service in early morning or at midnight should cost more than the reward during day time. If a higher reward is not offered for movement at this particular time, then the probability of participation is lower. We define the time coefficient TC_{t_i} to represent the significance of the time of day t_i. The time of day is quantized into four time intervals int_i, each lasting 6 h (i.e., $int_1 = [4$–$10)$ a.m., $int_2 = [10$ a.m.–4 p.m.), $int_3 = [4$–10 p.m.) and $int_4 = [10$ p.m.–4 a.m.)). Similarly, the day of week is categorized as either weekend or weekday. Our model assigns a higher time coefficient (i.e., $TC_{t_i} = 2$) to weekends if $t_i \in (int_1 \ or \ int_4)$ and weekday midnight if $t_i \in int_4$. For the rest of time intervals considering weekdays or weekends, TC_{t_i} is set to one.

  The reward points $r_{t_i}(sr_i)$ to be paid by the server to each hotspot provider to move to sr_i at time t_i is defined as:

$$r_{t_i}(sr_i) = \frac{\alpha \times D_{sr_i}}{1 + \beta \times SRE_{sr_i}} \times TC_{t_i} \times r_0 \qquad (5.5)$$

where r_0 is the standard reward point that is offered to all hotspot providers in oversupplied subregions for movement to undersupplied subregions to ensure the fairness among the subregions. SRE_{sr_i} and D_{sr_i} are the subregion entropy and spatio-temporal density of sr_i, respectively. α and β are, respectively, weights for D_{sr_i} and SRE_{sr_i} which are determined based on the market. TC_{t_i} is the time coefficient of the reward. The reward is simply proportional to the spatio-temporal density and time of day and reversely proportional to the subregion entropy. The constant "1" is needed to prevent division by zero.

5.4.3   Participation Probability Model

When a reward value of an undersupplied subregion is advertised to hotspot providers of oversupplied subregions, each provider decides whether or not to move to that undersupplied subregion. We introduce a simple participation probability model to determine the hotspot providers' willingness to response positively to a given reward. Each hotspot provider sp_i is characterized by a participation probability $p_{sp_i} \in [0, 1]$. The participation probability is time-dependent, i.e. it varies over an interval of time. For example, if the provider sp_i has participation probability x to move to sr_j from sr_k in time slot t_i, it may have participation probability y to move to sr_j in time slot t_j. To design the participation probability model, we consider two key sets of factors, incentive (e.g. reward value) and disincentive (e.g. travel cost and total credit account), which are paramount in the relative willingness to participate in a reward-based scheme [15]. Consequently, the participation probability model is defined based on two heuristics.

- *Spatial heuristic:* This spatial heuristic is based on the fact that incentives to migrate or relocate can be in some cases costly. For example, [15] shows that although the reward is the main incentive to participate, lack of flexibility in daily schedules or changing habits (e.g., changing their daily path) is the main reason to reject it. Since the benefit of incentive has trade-off against the travel distance in the decision process, our model considers travel cost as an indicator of how probable it is for a hotspot provider to move. The intuition is that a hotspot provider who is further away from a subregion is less likely to move. We calculate the travel cost as travel time between two subregions sr_i and sr_j, denoted by $tc(sr_i, sr_j)$ using Google Maps Distance matrix API.
- *Economic heuristic:* For each hotspot provider, we maintain a total account acc denotes the total earned credits up to t_i. The intuition is that a hotspot provider with a higher total credit account is less likely to be willing to earn more reward points than those with fewer credit points. For example, if a hotspot provider is a relatively new provider, the probability that it will move to an undersupplied subregion is higher than more established providers. This can be explained by the studies by [16] and [44] which demonstrate that participants with higher income are likely to be less sensitive to a marginal monetary incentive compared to participants with lower incomes. The *reward* value is also of paramount importance. The provider will also determine the reward in credits to move.

Fig. 5.5 An example of
participation model in the
time slot t_i

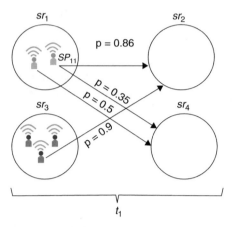

Given $tc(sr_i, sr_j)$, acc and *reward* value, the participation probability is modeled
based on three probability values $p_{\text{travel cost}}$, p_{account} and p_{reward}. We assume that
probability values $p_{\text{travel cost}}$, p_{account} and p_{reward} for hotspot provider sp_i in the time
slot t_i are derived from different distributions which can be obtained based on the
previous responses of the hotspot providers or it can be updated in real-time according to the providers responses to different reward offers. The probability distribution
values are assumed to be known a priori. For the sake of simplicity, we model the
participation probability of a hotspot provider based on the total account, travel cost
and reward value R in time slot t_i through the weighted-sum method as follows:

$$p_{t_i}(sp_i \rightarrow sr_j) = \frac{w_t \times p_{\text{travel cost}} + w_{acc} \times p_{\text{account}} + w_r \times p_{\text{reward}}}{p_{\text{travel cost}} + p_{\text{account}} + p_{\text{reward}}} \qquad (5.6)$$

where the weights w_t, w_{acc}, w_r which range from 0 to 1 reflect the importance
level of each factor, i.e., $p_{\text{travel cost}}$, p_{account} and p_{reward} respectively. Each hotspot
provider expresses their own preferences on factors by assigning values to the
weights. To demonstrate the applicability of the participation probability, we investigate the changes across the two different probability distributions: Uniform and
Gaussian distribution. Consequently, the participation probability model captures
a wide variety of incentive behaviors by varying different weights and parameters
generated by the probability distributions. Figure 5.5 shows an example of two
oversupplied subregions and two undersupplied subregions participation model. As
can be seen, the hotspot provider sp_{11} in sr_1 has the probability of 0.86 to move to
sr_2. Then, the *aggregated* value of participation probabilities P_{ij} is calculated as:

$$P_{ij} = \frac{1}{n} \sum_{k=1}^{n} p_{t_i}(sp_{ki} \rightarrow sr_j) \qquad (5.7)$$

where n is the surplus number of hotspot providers in the oversupplied subregion
sr_i that is computed based on the difference of the number of supplied N_s and

demanded providers N_d in sr_i. The number of hotspot providers who are interested to move from the oversupplied subregion sr_i to undersupplied subregion sr_j within the time slot t_i is determined based on P_{ij}.

A transition matrix $M_{n \times m}$ is constructed to represent the movement among subregions. Each row corresponds to an oversupplied subregion sr_i and each column corresponds to an undersupplied subregion sr_j. Each element m_{ij} in the matrix denotes the number of hotspot providers who are willing to move from an oversupplied subregion sr_i to an undersupplied subregion sr_j in time slot t_i which is computed as:

$$m_{ij} = P_{ij} \times \delta_i \tag{5.8}$$

where δ_i is the surplus number of hotspot providers of sr_i. For example, the surplus number of the oversupplied subregion sr_1 is 13 (i.e., $\delta_1 = 13$). Given the offered reward value for sr_4, the participation probability value of each of those 13 surplus providers are computed (e.g., in Fig. 5.5, $p_{t_i}(sp_{11} \rightarrow sr_4) = 0.35$). Then, P_{14} is determined based on Eq. 5.7 (e.g., $P_{14} = \frac{1}{13} \sum_{k=1}^{13} p_{t_i}(sp_{k1} \rightarrow sr_4) = 0.16$). The transition value in the transition matrix m_{14} is computed based on δ_1 and P_{14} i.e., $m_{14} = P_{14} \times \delta_1 = 0.16 \times 13 \simeq 2$. This means that only 2 hotspot providers of 13 providers are willing to move from sr_1 to sr_4 at t_i considering the reward value.

The transition matrix $M(t_i)$ is computed as follows:

$$M(t_i) = \begin{bmatrix} m_{ij} & \cdots & m_{im} \\ . & & . \\ m_{nj} & \cdots & m_{nm} \end{bmatrix} \tag{5.9}$$

5.4.4 Greedy Network Flow Algorithm for Crowdsourced Service Coverage Balancing Using the Incentive Model

We propose a greedy network flow based redistribution approach that offers incentives to redistribute the hotspot providers. The idea of the algorithm is to select appropriate crowdsourced hotspot service providers at every instance of time and assign them to subregions so that the equilibrium can be achieved (an assignment problem). The reason this approach is called "greedy" is that in every time slot, it only tries to find the equilibrium for the current assignment (i.e., local optimization instead of global optimization). Because hotspot providers arrive dynamically, it becomes challenging to achieve the global equilibrium. Since the system does not have prior knowledge about future hotspot providers, it tries to reach an equilibrium locally in every time slot. Therefore, the challenge is to perform the hotspot provider assignment in a given time slot with the goal of achieving the coverage equilibrium across the whole time period. We formulate the assignment problem as a flow network problem and find the matching of

---

Algorithm 7 Greedy Redistribute Algorithm

Input: An edgeless bipartite graph G (oversupplied subregions set OSR, undersupplied subregions set USR, $\varnothing$), edge set E based on transition matrix
Output: An assignment between oversupplied subregions and undersupplied subregions
1: **while** USR $\neq \varnothing$ and OSR $\neq \varnothing$ **do**   ▷ There is no undersupplied and oversupplied subregion available.
2:     (G,OSR,USR) = Initial Assignment(G,E)
3:     (AG,AOSR,AUSR) = Refinement(OSR,USR,G)
4:     assigned set = Assignment (AOSR,AUSR,AG)
5: **end while**
6: **Return** assigned set

---

oversupplied subregions and undersupplied subregions from the flow. We then divide the assignment into two phases: *initial assignment* and *refinement*. The *initial assignment* phase finds a matching for the set of oversupplied subregions and the set of undersupplied subregions. A hotspot provider is assigned to a subregion if they are matched with each other based on the transition matrix. The *refinement* phase then builds the corresponding flow network between the remaining oversupplied subregions' hotspot providers and undersupplied subregions' hotspot providers through calculating new assignments. Algorithm 7 gives the details of the greedy algorithm. In general, the greedy algorithm works in the following three steps: (a) initial assignment module, (b) refinement module, and (c) final assignment module.

5.4.4.1   Initial Assignment Module

To reach the coverage equilibrium, the first step is to assign hotspot providers from the oversupplied subregions to undersupplied subregions if their respective participation probability model supports such transitions. Given a set of oversupplied subregions $OSR_i = \{osr_1, osr_2, \ldots\}$ and a set of undersupplied subregions $USR_i = \{usr_1, usr_2, \ldots\}$ in the time slot t_i, we model the flow network as a bipartite residual graph $G = (OSR, USR, E)$ which is divided into two disjoint sets of vertices OSR and USR, i.e., OSR and USR are each independent. Each vertex osv in OSR represents an oversupplied subregion from where we may incentivize a hotspot provider to move. Each vertex usv in USR represents an undersupplied subregion that receives a hotspot provider from oversupplied subregions. Each edge $e = (osv, usv) \in E$ connects vertex osv in OSR to usv in USR which means that there is at least one hotspot provider who wants to move from the subregion osv to the subregion usv. Each edge has an associated flow value f_e representing the number of hotspot providers who are willing to move based on the transition matrix. Each vertex (i.e., subregion) has also a capacity value which is the total number of hotspot providers to move or receive. Noted that an edge's flow $f_{(osv,usv)}$ cannot exceed its capacity C_{osv}. We assign through two types of edges. First, we use any edge that has $f_{(osv,usv)} < C_{usv}$ and $C_{osv} > 0$ as a forward edge. Second, we use any edge to go backward from usv to osv if $f_{(osv,usv)} > 0$ as a

---

Algorithm 8 Initial Assignment(G,E)

Input: An edgeless bipartite graph G (oversupplied subregions set OSR,undersupplied subregions set USR, $\varnothing$), edge set E based on transition matrix

Output: An updated graph after initial assignment, oversupplied subregions set and undersupplied subregions set

1: **for** each edge $e_{(osv,usv)} \in E$ **do** ▷ It selects the edge in which C_{usv} is the maximum capacity.
2:     **if** $f_e < C_{osv}$ and $C_{usv} > 0$ and $C_{osv} > 0$ **then**
3:         **if** $C_{usv} > f_e$ **then**
4:             AddForwardEdge($osv, usv, 0, G$)
5:             AddBackwardEdge(usv, osv, f_e, G)
6:             $C_{osv} = C_{osv} - f_e$
7:             $C_{usv} = C_{usv} - f_e$
8:         **else**
9:             AddForwardEdge($osv, usv, f_e - C_{usv}, G$)
10:            AddBackwardEdge(usv, osv, C_{usv}, G)
11:            $C_{osv} = C_{osv} - C_{usv}$
12:            $C_{usv} = 0$
13:         **end if**
14:     **else**
15:         **if** $f_e \geqslant C_{osv}$ and $C_{usv} > 0$ and $C_{osv} > 0$ **then**
16:            **if** $C_{usv} > C_{osv}$ **then**
17:                AddForwardEdge($osv, usv, f_e - C_{osv}, G$)
18:                AddBackwardEdge(usv, osv, C_{osv}, G)
19:                $C_{osv} = 0$
20:                $C_{usv} = C_{usv} - C_{osv}$
21:            **else**
22:                AddForwardEdge($osv, usv, f_e - C_{usv}, G$)
23:                AddBackwardEdge(usv, osv, C_{usv}, G)
24:                $C_{osv} = C_{usv} - C_{osv}$
25:                $C_{usv} = 0$
26:            **end if**
27:         **end if**
28:     **end if**
29: **end for**
30: **return** G, OSR and USR

---

backward edge. The idea of using the residual graph is to keep track of remaining capacities and flow which we send through two types of edges. The details of the *initial assignment* algorithm are outlined in Algorithm 8.

Algorithm 8 starts with the set of edges extracted from the transition matrix. We use a heuristic to select the edge. Our heuristic selects the edge related to the highest undersupplied subregion. If the subregions usr_i, usr_j and usr_k have the highest, second highest and least shortages, we select the edge in which the end node is usr_i. For each edge $e = (osv, usv)$, it checks the capacity values of two oversupplied and undersupplied subregions C_{osv} and C_{usv}, respectively. If usv and osv still have available capacity, it will add a forward edge and update the residual flow value of the forward edge with respect to C_{osv} and C_{usv}. It then adds a backward edge $e(usv, osv)$ and sets the flow value of the backward edge by the exact number of hotspot providers who are moving from the subregion usv to osv

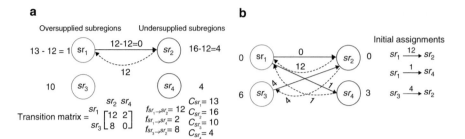

Fig. 5.6 Snapshots of a simple flow network for several iterations in the time slot t_i. (**a**) After the first iteration. (**b**) After the initial assignment

(Lines 2–28). Since flows in opposite directions counterbalance, decreasing the flow from the forward edge from osv to usv is the same as increasing the flow from usv to osv. If C_{osv} or C_{usv} is zero (i.e., no available capacity), e is not a valid edge to be added. The iteration terminates when there is no edge in the set E (i.e., there exists no mapping between OSR and USR).

Figure 5.6a shows the example of the corresponding flow network from Fig. 5.5. In Fig. 5.6a, we pick the edge $sr_1 \rightarrow sr_2$, because sr_2 has the highest shortage. The flow value along the edge is 12 which means that we could send 12 hotspot providers along this edge from sr_1 to sr_2. We then check the capacity of sr_1 and sr_2 which are 13 and 16 respectively. Since they have available capacity, we add the edge $sr_1 \rightarrow sr_2$ and decrease the flow of the edge by 12. We then add a backward edge $sr_2 \rightarrow sr_1$ (denoted by dashed line) and set its flow value to 12. The capacity of sr_1 and sr_2 also decrease by 12.

5.4.4.2   Refinement Module

Once we complete the initial assignment phase for those subregions with the assigned hotspot providers, we check the capacity values of all subregions in OSR and USR. If there are any spaces and hotspot providers available in both undersupplied and oversupplied subregions, we will attend to the refinement phase. We calculate new assignments among the remaining hotspot providers of oversupplied and undersupplied subregions. Let us assume that the set of these remaining oversupplied subregions and undersupplied subregions are called $ROSR$ and $RUSR$ (Algorithm 9, Lines 1–2). In this regard, the algorithm does a DFS to find a valid path from $rov \in ROSR$ to any $ruv \in RUSR$. A path is valid if the minimum flow of all edges is greater than zero. It then sends the flow along a path still having capacity. It might erase some flow that we had previously assigned through pushing backwards. Note that there can be a path from rov to ruv in the residual network, even though there is no path from rov to ruv in the original network, due to adding forward and backward edges in the initial assignment phase. The time complexity of refinement module is exponential due to the need to compute

---

Algorithm 9 Refinement(OSR, USR, G)

Input: oversupplied subregions set OSR, undersupplied subregions set USR and a bipartite graph G (OSR,USR, E') after the initial assignment

Output: The updated graph G based on assignments between oversupplied subregions and undersupplied subregions, updated oversupplied subregion list $ROSR$ and updated $ROSR$ undersupplied subregion list

1:   $ROSR = \{rov, rov \in OSR$ and $C_{rov} > 0\}$ ▷ The list of oversupplied subregions have
     remaining capacity after the initial assignment.

2:   $RUSR = \{ruv, ruv \in USR, C_{ruv} > 0\}$ ▷ The list of undersupplied subregions have
     remaining capacity after the initial assignment.

3:   **for** each $rov \in ROSR$ **do**

4:      **for** each $ruv \in RUSR$ **do**

5:         pathSet = find-all-shortest-path(rov, ruv)   ▷ find all shortest path between rov and
    ruv.

6:         **for** each path $p \in$ pathSet **do**

7:            validPath = true

8:            **for** each edge $e \in p$ **do**

9:               **if** $f_e < o$ **then**

10:                  validPath = false

11:                  break

12:               **end if**

13:            **end for**

14:            **if** validPath = true **then**

15:               update (G) ▷ Push the flow through updating the forward and backward edges
    and capacities of rov and ruv.

16:               break

17:            **end if**

18:         **end for**

19:         **if** $C_{rov} = 0$ **then**

20:            remove rov from $ROSR$ and G and update forward and backward edges

21:         **end if**

22:         **if** $C_{ruv} = 0$ **then**

23:            remove ruv from $RUSR$ and G and update forward and backward edges

24:         **end if**

25:      **end for**

26: **end for**

27: **return** $G, ROSR, RUSR$

---

a large number of time-consuming path finding. Algorithm 9 represents the details of the *refinement*.

After completing the initial assignment process, we will obtain Fig. 5.6b which is not the optimal solution. In Fig. 5.6b, sr_3 has six hotspot providers left and sr_4 has a shortage of three hotspot providers. By doing a DFS, we will find the path $sr_3 \rightarrow sr_2 \rightarrow sr_1 \rightarrow sr_4$ denoted by the red edges. We interpret the path as follows. First, sr_3 sends the flow of 1 (*i.e., the minimum flow along the path*) along $sr_3 \rightarrow sr_2$ and there are no more forward edges going away from sr_2 toward sr_4 that have available flow. Therefore, we push back the flow along ($sr_2 \rightarrow sr_1$), i.e., some units of flow that came along ($sr_1 \rightarrow sr_2$) can now be taken over by flow coming into sr_1 along ($sr_2 \rightarrow sr_1$). After pushing back the flow to sr_1, we send the

Fig. 5.7 Refinement phase of
Fig. 5.6

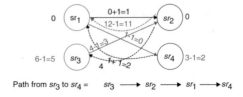

Path from sr_3 to sr_4 = $sr_3 \longrightarrow sr_2 \longrightarrow sr_1 \longrightarrow sr_4$

Algorithm 10 Assignment($AOSR, AUSR, AG$)

Input: Assigned oversupplied subregions set $AOSR$, assigned undersupplied subregions set $AUSR$ and assigned bipartite graph AG (AOSR,AUSR, AE') after refinement
Output: Final assignment between oversupplied subregions and undersupplied subregions

1: **for** each $ov \in AOSR$ **do**
2:     **for** each edge $e \in AG$ **do**
3:         **if** $e.endNode = ov$ **then**
4:             compute $acceptedFlow$ ▷ calculate the number of hotspot providers in subregion ov that accepts the reward to move from $e.endNode$ to $e.startNode$.
5:             $f_e = acceptedFlow$ ▷ Update the flow of the backward edge
6:             update (AG) ▷ Update the flow of the forward edge and capacities C_{ov} and C_{uv} based on the acceptedFlow.
7:         **end if**
8:     **end for**
9: **end for**
10: **return** the final assignment

---

flow of 1 through $sr_1 \rightarrow sr_4$. While doing so, we also update the graph. We simply increase flow on forward edges and decrease flow on backward edges (see Fig. 5.7).

5.4.4.3   Assignment Module

If a hotspot provider is selected and accepts the reward, it moves toward the particular undersupplied subregion. After providing the service in that subregion, the hotspot provider receives the reward via the system. In this case, the hotspot provider is no longer part of the initial subregion. In an ideal case, all hotspot providers will accept the offer and move. However, it is not practical due to the participation probability. Therefore, our optimization goal is to achieve coverage equilibrium in each time slot t_i.

The *greedy redistribute algorithm* tries to achieve the coverage balance in an iterative process where in each time slot t_i a selected number of hotspot providers in the oversupplied subregions accept and move to undersupplied subregions (Algorithm 7, Line 4). In each iteration, the algorithm aims to minimize the number of undersupplied hotspot providers until there is no undersupplied and oversupplied subregion available (Algorithm 7, Line 1).

After the refinement process, for each assignment (i.e., backward edge), the assigned oversupplied hotspot providers decide whether or not to accept the offer (Algorithm 10, Lines 1–4). Based on the number of accepted assignments, the flow

Fig. 5.8 The number of supplied or demanded hotspot providers in each subregion after applying the incentive-based approach

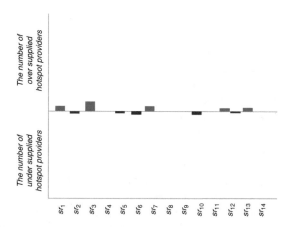

of the corresponding backward and forward edges, shortage and surplus values are then updated (Algorithm 10, Lines 5–6). Figure 5.8 shows the distribution histogram of Fig. 5.3 after applying an incentive-based approach.

5.5 Experiment Results

We conduct five sets of experiments. These experiments show (1) the effectiveness of our approach to reach equilibrium: (2) the scalability of our approach over different distributions to investigate how the execution time and the number of time slots varies as the problem becomes larger: (3) the effectiveness of our approach in comparison with a baseline approach: (4) the effect of the participation probability in terms of the execution time and the number of time slots and (5) the effect of varying acceptance ratio on the proposed approach.

5.5.1 Experiment Setup

Datasets There exist different frameworks for WiFi on taxis and Uber in the real world. For example, in Scotland and London, City Cabs taxis[2] and CabWiFi[3] offer free on-board WiFi service, respectively. The uberWIFI turns Ubers' cars into a moving WiFi hotspot in Philadelphia[4] As a result, the use of *Uber* and *taxi cab* datasets is reasonable and realistic in the context of this research.

---

[2]www.citycabs.co.uk.

[3]www.cabwifi.com.

[4]www.uber.com/blog/philadelphia/take-work-on-the-gowith-uberwifi.

The *taxi* dataset contains mobility traces of 536 taxi cabs in San Francisco BAY Area, USA collected over 30 days which is fairly dense [122]. Each line of traces contains latitude, longitude, occupancy and time. The occupancy shows if a cab is occupied (i.e., 1) or free (i.e., 0). The location-updates are quite fine-grained and the average time interval between two consecutive location updates is less than 10 s. As a result, we can generate a denser sample of instantaneous hotspot locations. For our experiments, we define each sampled GPS point of an occupied cab as a hotspot provider and a free cab as a hotspot user (i.e., 10,946,098 location points in total). We divide San Francisco (i.e., region) to several subregions based on the zip code that represents a subregion and there are 84 subregions in this case. Based on extracted supply and demand values, there are 56 undersupplied subregions and 28 oversupplied subregions.

Uber is a ride-sharing company where those who need a ride are linked to those who are willing to drive. We have used an *Uber* dataset that contains 25K anonymized GPS traces from black car pickups in San Francisco produced in January 2007.[5] Line in each trace is spaced at about 4 s apart. Similar to taxi dataset, we use zip codes to divide San Francisco into several subregions, which is 66 in this case. For our experiments, we assume that each GPS point is either a hotpot service provider or user and there are 1,111,513 location points in total. We consider 33 undersupplied subregions and 33 oversupplied subregions in the Uber dataset.

We use an *extrapolated taxi* dataset which is generated based on the relationships among surplus or shortage of taxi services (S), population (P) and traffic volume (T) in the given geo location (i.e., San Francisco) to evaluate the scalability of our approach. Two new datasets, i.e., population[6] and traffic[7] in San Francisco SF are used with the Taxi cab dataset in the extrapolation process. We fit the datasets in R and run polynomial regression ($(lm(s\ A + xP + y + T^2))$) considering S as a dependent variable and P and T as independent variables. Here, *lm* is regression model in R, A is the intercept coefficient and x and y are coefficient of P and T respectively. The regression analysis generates the following fitted equations.

- For over-supplied postcodes: $S = 370.89 + 0.3594 * P - 0.2594 * T^2$
- For under-supplied postcodes: $S = 875 + 0.529 * P + 0.1156 * T^2$

Once the model is generated, the new extrapolated dataset is easily derived using the population dataset and traffic in SF and surrounding of SF (i.e., zip codes from San Francisco to Los Angeles). The extrapolated taxi dataset include 115 oversupplied subregions, 85 undersupplied subregions and 3,008,155 hotspot providers in total.

---

[5]http://www.infochimps.com/datasets/uber-anonymized-gps-logs.

[6]https://s3.amazonaws.com/SplitwiseBlogJB/2010+Census+Population+By+Zipcode+(ZCTA). csv.

[7]https://data.sfgov.org/Transportation/Estimated-Yearly-Pedestrian-Volume-at-Intersection/v62e-2jxp.

To the best of our knowledge, there are limited research investigating incentive based spatio-temporal coverage balance. We compare the proposed Greedy Redistribute Algorithm (GRA) and a greedy baseline algorithm to show the effectiveness of our approach.

- *BaseLine (BL):* In the BL approach, each hotspot provider is characterized by a participation probability to determine the provider's willingness to participate. The participation probability model depends on several factors including the reward value (i.e., incentive), travel cost and the total account. The participation probability model is transformed into the transition matrix which specifies the number of providers who are willing to move from an oversupplied subregion to an undersupplied subregion. Hotspot providers are randomly selected from the oversupplied subregions and assigned to undersupplied subregions if they are matched according to the transition matrix in each iteration. The process stops when there is no undersupplied or oversupplied subregion available. We treat BL as a greedy approach because it fills up the undersupplied subregions quickly considering hotspot providers from randomly-selected oversupplied subregions.
- *Greedy Redistribute Algorithm (GRA):* The proposed greedy algorithm in which the refinement phase (redistribution of initial assignments considering all subregions) and initial assignment heuristic (i.e., first select the edge related to the highest undersupplied subregion) are applied in each iteration (Algorithm 1).

The travel cost between two subregions are calculated using Google Maps Distance Matrix API that provides travel distance and time duration based on a recommended route that take traffic conditions into account. We use the default travel mode (i.e., car driving) and departure time (i.e., current time). Given the travel time tc, the probability value $p_{travel\ cost}$ is calculated. The $p_{account}$ and p_{reward} are uniformly selected within a range of $[0, 1]$. For each time slot, we generate an $m \times n$ transition matrix. m and n denote the number of oversupplied and undersupplied subregion, respectively. We generate $\frac{m \times n}{2}$ transitions from randomly-selected sr_i, $i \in [1, m]$ to sr_j, $j \in [1, n]$. For example, 784 transitions are generated in a taxi transition matrix 56×28. The number of hotspot providers who are willing to move from oversupplied subregion sr_i to sr_j is computed as $P_{ij} \times \delta_i$ for $i \in [1, m]$ in each transition. For example, if the aggregated participation P_{14} is 0.5 in a randomly selected transition from sr_1 to sr_4 and the number of oversupplied hotspot providers of sr_1 is 20 (i.e., $\delta_1 = 20$), then the transition value is 10. This means that only 10 hotspot providers are willing to move from sr_1 to sr_4. The default assignment ratio in each time slot is uniformly selected within a range of $[0.4, 0.7]$. Here, 0.4 means that at each iteration only 40% of the hotspot providers agrees to move from sr_i to sr_j. Therefore, if the assigned flow from sr_i to sr_j is ten hotspot providers, only four providers accept the reward to move. The remaining parameters are also randomly generated using the uniform distribution. We run our experiments on an Intel Core i7 CPU at 3.40 GHZ with 8 GB of RAM under Windows 10. All the algorithms are implemented in Python. All experiments are repeated 100 times and the average results are computed. The transition matrix is randomly generated in each run.

5.5.2   Reaching Equilibrium Using the Incentive Model

According to Definition 17, we consider a region to be in equilibrium when there
is no shortage of providers in any subregion. In the first experiment, we explore the
effectiveness of the proposed incentive model to reach equilibrium in two different
scenarios. In the first scenario, we consider around 474,000 shortage of providers in
33 undersupplied subregions on the Uber dataset in the time slot t_1.

Figure 5.9 depicts the distribution trend and actual values of the shortage of
providers in each time slot. The proposed incentive model gradually reduces the
shortage of providers and we reach equilibrium, i.e., empty distribution of shortage
in the time slot t_{17}. The rate of shortage reduction is higher in earlier time slots
(t_2, t_3, t_4 and t_5) and lower when close to the equilibrium as time slot t_{16} and t_{17} has
similar distribution pattern.

In the second scenario, similar to the first scenario, the proposed incentive model
gradually reduces the shortage of providers in undersupplied subregions (Fig. 5.10).
However, we could not reach equilibrium as around 74,000 shortage of providers
from initial 474,000 remain in the undersupplied regions in time slot t_{17} because
the distribution of surplus providers becomes zero. Therefore, equilibrium is not
reached due to the shortage of surplus hotspot providers in oversupplied subregions.

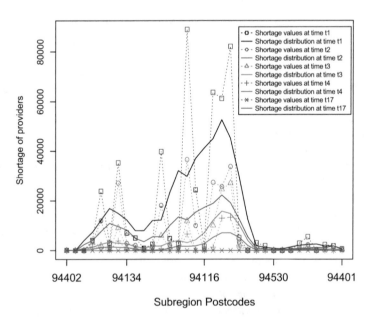

Fig. 5.9 Distributions reaching equilibrium in undersupplied subregions

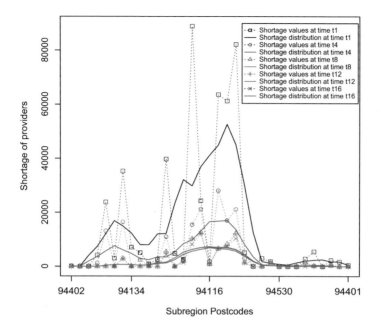

Fig. 5.10 Not reaching equilibrium in undersupplied subregions

5.5.3   The Scalability of the Proposed Approach

In the second set of experiments, we evaluate the scalability of our proposed approach by varying the edge density of the graph (i.e., number of transitions) from 20 to 80% with an iteration range of 20 while the values of other parameters remain constant. We measure the edge density of the graph as the ratio between the number of existing edges and the number of possible edges in the corresponding complete bipartite graph. For example, the number of edges for 20% density of Taxi graph is $\frac{28 \times 56}{5} \simeq 314$.

Figure 5.11 depicts the execution time to reach equilibrium of our proposed approach on taxi, Uber and extrapolated taxi datasets when the edge density varies. As expected, for each dataset, the execution time increases as the graph becomes denser. We conclude that the proposed algorithm is scalable for a larger number of subregions, hotspot providers and transitions (e.g., less than 2.3 s for 200 subregions, 80% density i.e., 7820 transitions and 3,008,155 hotspot providers). Figure 5.12 shows the number of time slots to reach equilibrium for our three datasets as the edge density varies. The slight difference (i.e., only one time slot) shows the proposed approach is stable in different distributions of data in terms of subregions, hotspot providers and the graph density.

Fig. 5.11 Execution time vs. edge density

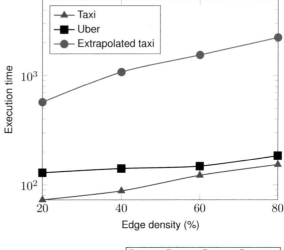

Fig. 5.12 No. of time slots vs. edge density

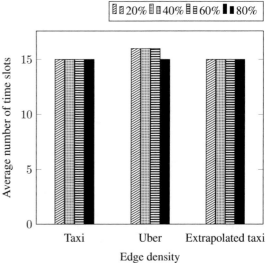

5.5.4   *The Effectiveness of the Proposed Approach*

In the third set of experiments, we study the effectiveness of the proposed GRA algorithm by comparing with the baseline algorithm BL. We use the static transition matrix through each experiment for more objective comparison. If the algorithms cannot reach equilibrium after maximum 1000 time slots (a relatively large number), the algorithm will stop. Table 5.2 summarizes the number of completed run out of 100 times for both algorithms on three datasets by varying the edge density of the graph from 20 to 80% with an iteration range of 20 while the values of other parameters remain constant. The results show that GRA significantly outperforms

Table 5.2 Total number of completed run

Algorithm	Taxi				Uber				Extrapolated taxi			
	20%	40%	60%	80%	20%	40%	60%	80%	20%	40%	60%	80%
BL	0	59	97	100	0	1	5	50	68	100	100	100
GRA	11	100	100	100	17	33	81	100	99	100	100	100

Table 5.3 Execution time vs. edge density

Algorithm	Taxi				Uber				Extrapolated taxi			
	20%	40%	60%	80%	20%	40%	60%	80%	20%	40%	60%	80%
BL	0.234	0.147	0.079	0.097	0.222	0.218	0.214	0.162	0.484	0.706	1.106	1.522
GRA	4.09	0.093	0.135	0.168	1.812	1.433	0.317	0.111	0.658	1.014	1.587	2.139

BL algorithm. This indicates that the refinement phase in GRA algorithm plays an important role to reach equilibrium specifically when the graph is sparser. For example, for the Uber dataset, compared with BL, the number of completed run is 76 and 50% better for 60 and 80% dense graph. When the graph is highly dense, for taxi and extrapolated taxi, the number of completed run by two algorithms are close. The reason is when the graph is denser, there are a lot of transitions to reach equilibrium. Table 5.3 reports the computation time of both the GRA and BL algorithm. In terms of computation time, GRA is less efficient approach due to its high computation time of computing a large number of time consuming shortest path operations in the refinement phase. To conclude, the GRA algorithm is practical for real application when the graph is sparser.

5.5.5 Effect of Participation Probability Model

The fourth set of experiments investigates the effect of participation probability parameters (see Eq. 5.6) on GRA approach on our three different datasets. For this experiment, we vary the weight values to show the importance of each probability parameter as follows: $[w_{tt} = 0.1, w_{acc} = 0.1, w_r = 0.8]$ for p_{reward}, $[w_{tt} = 0.8, w_{acc} = 0.1, w_r = 0.1]$ for $p_{travel\ cost}$ and $[w_{tt} = 0.1, w_{acc} = 0.8, w_r = 0.1]$ for $p_{account}$. We also fix the edge density as 40%, acceptance ratio as [40–70%]. In the first experiment, we measure the effect of p_{reward} (i.e., reward value) on the participation of hotspot providers. To demonstrate the applicability of the p_{reward}, we investigate the changes of p_{reward} across two different probability distribution: Uniform and Gaussian distribution. First, we assume that the low and high p_{reward} values are uniformly distributed between [0.1–0.3] and [0.7–0.9], respectively. Figure 5.13a depicts the influence of high and low p_{reward} on the total number of time slots to achieve equilibrium. The results show that the total number of time slots decreases dramatically as p_{reward} increases. This is because a larger value of reward means more providers are willing to participate in the movement. The lower p_{reward} leads to an exponential increase in taxi and extrapolated taxi datasets due to

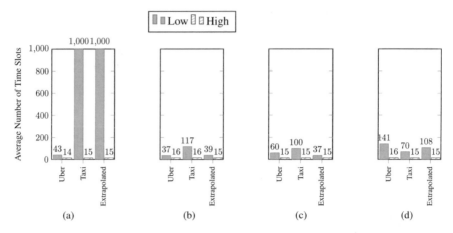

Fig. 5.13 No. of time slots vs. participation probability. (**a**) p_{reward} uniform. (**b**) p_{reward} normal. (**c**) $p_{account}$. (**d**) $p_{travel\ cost}$

not achieving equilibrium in all runs and terminating after 1000 time slots. In the second experiment, we assume that the p_{reward} values are normally distributed. We vary the mean μ and standard deviation σ values for the change. Specifically, we consider the truncated normal distribution of probabilities over $[0, 1]$, with μ and σ. We set ($\mu = 0.2$, $\sigma = 0.1$) and ($\mu = 0.8$, $\sigma = 0.1$) to measure the impact of *low* and *high* p_{reward}, respectively. Figure 5.13b illustrates the impact of the reward on the number of time slots to reach equilibrium. As can be seen, a higher p_{reward} has a positive effect on the decision to participate and consequently leads to a significant decrease in the number of time slots (e.g., decreasing from 117 to 16 time slots when increasing the reward in taxi dataset). Therefore, the impact of the reward is significant in both uniform and normal distributions in all datasets. In the third and fourth sets of experiments, we also assume that $p_{travel\ cost}$ and $p_{account}$ values are normally distributed. For example, to measure the effect of low total account, we consider the truncated normal distribution of $p_{account}$ with ($\mu = 0.2$, $\sigma = 0.1$). We also set $w_{tt} = 0.1$, $w_{acc} = 0.8$ and $w_r = 0.1$. Figure 5.13c, d shows how $p_{account}$ and $p_{travel\ cost}$ affect the number of time slots to reach equilibrium, respectively. We observe that both $p_{account}$ and $p_{travel\ cost}$ have significant influences on decreasing the total number of time slots to reach coverage equilibrium.

5.5.6 Effect of Acceptance Ratio

The last set of experiments evaluates the effect of varying acceptance ratio on GRA approach. For this experiment, we fix the edge density as 40%, $w_{tt} = 0.1$, $w_{acc} = 0.1$ and $w_r = 0.8$. We vary the acceptance ratio which is uniformly selected within the following ranges: *low* = [20–40%] and *high* = [70–90%]. For each range of acceptance ratio, we consider the *low*, *medium* and *high* p_{reward} which follow a

Table 5.4 No. of time slots vs. acceptance ratio

	Low p_{reward}			Medium p_{reward}			High p_{reward}		
	Taxi	Uber	Extrapolated	Taxi	Uber	Extrapolated	Taxi	Uber	Extrapolated
Low acceptance ratio	1000	1000	1000	1000	1000	1000	1000	1000	1000
High acceptance ratio	79	10	24	8	9	8	8	9	8

normal distribution as ($\mu = 0.2$, $\sigma = 0.1$), ($\mu = 0.5$, $\sigma = 0.2$) and ($\mu = 0.8$, $\sigma = 0.1$), respectively. For brevity, we only vary p_{reward} parameter ($p_{travel\ cost}$ and $p_{account}$ show similar trends as observed in the previous experiments). Table 5.4 depicts the effect of acceptance ratio on the number of time slots on three datasets. As expected, a higher acceptance ratio obtains the lower number of time slots to reach equilibrium. As can be seen, the decrease rate becomes larger with a higher reward (e.g., 79 time slots for low reward and 8 time slots for high reward in taxi dataset). This can be explained through significant willingness for a higher reward value. As a result, more hotspot providers are interested to move and the number of accepted assignments is higher. The results also show that when the acceptance ratio is low, the GRA algorithm does not achieve equilibrium and stops after 1000 time slots, regardless of the p_{reward}. This can be explained based on the fact that a really low acceptance ratio results in an insufficient number of hotspot providers who accept the assignment and move in each iteration. To conclude, by comparing Table 5.4 and Fig. 5.13b with the medium acceptance ratio of [40–70%], we observe that the acceptance ratio contributes mostly to the improvement in terms of the number of time slots to achieve the coverage balance. The reward mostly has an impact when the acceptance ratio is relatively above average.

5.6   Chapter Summary

This chapter proposed a novel incentive-based greedy redistribution approach to achieve an optimal geographically-balanced coverage by offering incentives to crowdsourced hotspot service providers. The proposed approach is based on a new spatio-temporal incentive model that considers multiple parameters including location entropy, time of the day and spatio-temporal density to encourage the participation of crowdsourced service providers. We presented a new greedy network flow algorithm that offers incentives to redistribute the crowdsourced service providers to improve the crowdsourced coverage balance along an area. A novel participation probability model was also introduced to estimate the expected number of crowdsourced service providers movement based on spatio-temporal features. In our experiments, we demonstrated the scalability and effectiveness of our proposed approach to reach coverage equilibrium using two real datasets Uber and taxi. The results show that our greedy network flow algorithm has a satisfying scalability in terms of the number of time slots and execution time.

Chapter 6
Conclusion

Sensor cloud is an emerging field that provides unique storage and processing capabilities and opportunities, particularly for the use of a large amount of real-time sensor data streaming collected from all types of sensors and mobile devices such as smartphones. However, efficient and real-time delivery of sensor data is challenging. In this book, we have proposed a novel service framework to manage crowd-sourced sensor data focusing on spatio-temporal aspects while providing a balanced distribution of crowdsourcing providers. The service framework aims to provide a high-level abstraction (i.e., sensor cloud services) to model sensor data from functional and non-functional perspectives, seamlessly turning raw data into "ready to go" services. The proposal focused on spatio-temporal selection and composition of crowdsourced sensor cloud services. This is a new and novel direction in service-oriented computing research. In what follows, we recap the research objectives mentioned in the introduction. We also summarize the major contributions of this book. Finally, we discuss several possible future research directions.

6.1 Research Objectives Revisited

This section summarizes the research objectives, proposed methods and findings of this book.

- **To design and develop a service framework for cloud-based sensor data.** Chapter 3 defined a service-oriented framework to effectively and efficiently capture, manage and deliver cloud-based sensed data as user-desired services, taking into account users' spatio-temporal and qualitative requirements. We used a typical public transport scenario as our motivating scenario. We focused on modelling sensor cloud services based on the spatio-temporal features of sensor data, i.e., sensor data shared in a cloud can be abstracted as sensor cloud services. The functional attributes of sensor cloud services capture their spatio-temporal

© Springer International Publishing AG, part of Springer Nature 2018
A. Ghari Neiat, A. Bouguettaya, *Crowdsourcing of Sensor Cloud Services*,
https://doi.org/10.1007/978-3-319-91536-4_6

features and non-functional attributes describe their qualitative aspects. The functional attributes include service ID, a set of sensors that collect sensor data related to the service, space-time and the function offered by the service (e.g., modes of transportation). The space is presented by a line segment including the GPS start and end-points. The time shows start-time and end-time of the service. We also designed a service organization to efficiently search and select sensor cloud services. We devised a spatio-temporal index structure based on a 3D R-tree to efficiently and effectively access for sensor cloud services. QoS attributes are typically used to select functionality equivalent services. We introduced new QoS attributes, namely service time, freshness and accuracy, which focus on the dynamic aspects of the services. Service time reflects the expected time in minutes between the start and end points. Freshness measures how fresh the sensor data related to the service is. Accuracy indicates how a service is assured.

- **To devise QoS-aware spatio-temporal composition of sensor cloud services.** The research challenge is to select the "best" spatio-temporal composition of sensor cloud services within a range of users' requirements and QoS expectations. In Chap. 3, we modelled the spatio-temporal linear composition problem as a directed spatio-temporal graph search problem. In that graph, each vertex has an associated space-time attribute of a line segment service and each edge is associated with the QoS attributes. We proposed a spatio-temporal linear composition algorithm, using a modified version of the A* shortest path algorithm as the basis for finding the optimal linear composition plan. We also introduced the notion of a linear composability model to cater for checking that two line segment sensor cloud services are spatio-temporally composable. The initial composition plan needs to be replanned to prevent failures caused by a fluctuating QoS when the user executes the composed sensor cloud service. We developed a failure-proof mechanism based on the incremental replanning algorithm D* Lite to repair the linear composition plan when new information about the environment is received. The experimental results showed that this linear composition outperformed the spatio-temporal Dijkstra algorithm which was developed for our experiments. We also showed that a similar computation time was achieved in the failure-proof composition approach regardless of varying the QoS fluctuation ratio.

- **To design a crowdsourcing platform for real-time and adaptive service provisioning**. We designed a two-level spatio-temporal composition algorithm based on the proposed framework for the spatio-temporal linear composition of sensor cloud services, in Chap. 4. This two-level composition approach maps crowdsourced coverage as a QoS for selecting the optimal linear composition plan. Even more significantly, we considered the crowdsourced coverage as a region service itself for each candidate linear plan. We then reformulated the problem of selecting a linear composition plan with the best crowdsourced coverage as selecting the best composed region services along the linear composition plans. In the case of crowdsourced region services, we also defined new quality parameters including signal strength, capacity and level of composability. The signal strength is modelled based on the distance between the region service and a user using the exponential attenuation probabilistic coverage model [11]. The capacity is the maximum amount of data that can be transmitted. We modelled the capacity based on the Signal to Noise Ratio Shannon-Hartley theorem [130]. The level of composability presents the number of available spatio-temporal neighbour region services. We also proposed two different approaches to this two-level service composition. The first approach considered *one path at a time* for selecting the best coverage along each and every optimal linear composition plan. The second approach considered *one segment at a time* for selecting the best coverage along every line segment service. We then proposed the QoS-aware spatio-temporal overlay composition approach in the scenario of WiFi hotspot sharing. In the experiments, we studied the scalability of both approaches in terms of execution time. The *one path at a time* approach applies a filtering mechanism to prune the search space to improve the efficiency of the overlay composition process. The experimental results showed that applying this filtering stage significantly reduces the computation time. In addition, we found that the new heuristic in the *one segment at a time* approach had a significant impact on the execution time and finding more accurate composition plans in terms of QoS cost.

- **To devise an incentive model to drive coverage of crowdsourced sensor cloud services**. Chapter 5 outlined a new spatio-temporal incentive-based approach to achieve a required coverage of crowdsourced services in a predefined region. We first proposed a spatio-temporal incentive model to encourage movement from oversupplied subregions to undersupplied subregions. The incentive model was defined based on the spatio-temporal dynamicity of the environment including changes in regional density, time of day and subregion entropy. We then introduced a new participation probability model to estimate the number of crowdsourced service providers who are moving to earn the offered incentive. We then formulated the problem of the crowdsourced providers' assignment as a flow network problem. A greedy flow network redistribution algorithm was proposed to redistribute the crowdsourced service providers through offering incentives. This algorithm aimed to select the appropriate crowdsourced service providers from oversupplied subregions in a particular time slot and to assign them to undersupplied subregions so that the required coverage can be attained. The conducted experiments presented the effectiveness and scalability of our greedy approach to reach a coverage balance of crowdsourced services using two real datasets (i.e., mobility traces of Uber and Taxi Cabs in San Francisco, USA). The experimental results also showed that the algorithm is scalable for larger numbers of subregions and hotspot providers and dense graph. Furthermore, we demonstrated that our approach is more effective in comparison to a baseline approach to reach equilibrium over different distributions.

6.2 Future Research

In this section, we identify and describe some future research directions.

6.2.1   Leveraging Crowdsourced Sensors for Real-Time Spatio-Temporal Linear Composition

In this book, we made the assumption that the linear service composition is created using services modelled by fixed sensors. Similarly, the QoS properties are modelled based on these historical sensors information. In future research, crowdsourced sensors may be considered as providing an alternative source of information to find a set of optimal linear composition plans from source point to destination point. This study could be extended to develop a set of new spatio-temporal selection and linear composition techniques to create an optimal linear composition plan using crowdsourced sensors to provide real-time sensor data about the quality of a sensor cloud service (e.g., bus or train). This could also be applied to obtaining feedback on the completeness of our present proposed approaches and comparing the crowdsourced and static sensors to augment reliability. Identifying and accessing the right sensors from the cloud which may be applicable to the current service is another interesting direction for future research. This is important as sensors will move from one mode of transportation to another, i.e., they would serve different sets of services at different locations and times. Developing efficient techniques to accurately identify sensors that will be mapped to the right service is another important area for future research.

6.2.2   Designing QoS-Aware Frameworks for Spatio-Temporal Selection and Composition of Transient Crowdsourced Services

We identify four different types of crowdsourced services which are modelled by considering *permanent* and *transient* in space and *deterministic* or *non-deterministic* in time. Crowdsourced services may be *spatially permanent* or *transient*. A *permanent* crowdsourced service is assumed to be fixed in space for the time required by a specific user. For example, John would like to share his WiFi hotspot while he is sitting in a cafe. A *transient* crowdsourced service is not tied to any specific location or any specific time. We assume that John may share his WiFi hotspot and also move from one location to another. In the case of permanent hotspot sharing, we assume that once a hotspot is part of a plan, that hotspot will not change its availability at a spatial location during the provision of the service. However, in the case of transient hotspot sharing, no such promise is given regarding the availability or spatial location of the hotspot. Additionally, crowdsourced services may also be *temporally deterministic* or *temporally non-deterministic*. *Temporally deterministic* refers to a crowdsourced service whose time of availability at a certain location is known and fixed in advance. Conversely, *temporally non-deterministic* refers to a crowdsourced service whose time availability is not known in advance.

In this book, we modelled permanent deterministic crowdsourced services. In future, we intend to extend our research on transient non-deterministic crowdsourced services. Since the transient services are represented by moving sensors, it is important that they be modelled in such a way that they are identified accordingly. This is important as clearly identifying the moving service allows for accurate and efficient composition of crowdsourced coverage. This also calls for new trajectory clustering techniques like convoys [72], flocks [149] and travelling companions [140] to efficiently discover the transient crowdsourced services. In addition, we suggest designing composition techniques for transient services which focus on efficiently discovering services with similar trajectories to users' trajectories.

In our current work, we assumed that QoS features of component services were deterministic relative to the crowdsourced sensor cloud services they were used for. Investigating the use of supervised or unsupervised approaches including Hidden Markov Model (HMM), Artificial Neural Networks (ANN) and Autoregressive Integrated Moving Average (ARIMA)[21] for spatio-temporal QoS prediction without prior knowledge is another interesting direction for future research.

6.2.3 Developing Dynamic Incentive Models

In this book, we assumed an off-line approach that considers a static population of crowdsourced service providers during the redistribution process. Our future research will extend the current framework to deal with the on-line arrival of both service providers and customers. Few studies to date have explored dynamic pricing models that can allocate tasks to participants on their arrival [14, 134, 135]. In this study, the coordinator of each subregion was assumed to decide the incentive value without negotiating with crowdsourced service providers. However, further investigation would examine how to integrate bid-price auction into the design of the incentive model. In particular, an automatic bid price decision process based on historical bid prices of providers can also be designed to decrease disturbance to service providers.

References

1. Nimbits data logging cloud sever.
2. Pachube feed cloud service.
3. Mahdi Abdelguerfi, Julie Givaudan, Kevin Shaw, and Roy Ladner. The 2-3tr-tree, a trajectory-oriented index structure for fully evolving valid-time spatio-temporal datasets. In *Proceedings of the 10th ACM international symposium on Advances in geographic information systems*, pages 29–34. ACM, 2002.
4. Karl Aberer, Manfred Hauswirth, and Ali Salehi. A middleware for fast and flexible sensor network deployment. In *Proceedings of the 32nd international conference on Very large data bases*, pages 1199–1202. VLDB Endowment, 2006.
5. Khandakar Ahmed and Mark Gregory. Integrating wireless sensor networks with cloud computing. In *2011 Seventh International Conference on Mobile Ad-hoc and Sensor Networks (MSN)*, pages 364–366. IEEE, 2011.
6. Ian F Akyildiz and Mehmet Can Vuran. *Wireless sensor networks*, volume 4. John Wiley & Sons, 2010.
7. Hussein Al-Helal and Rose Gamble. Introducing replaceability into web service composition. *IEEE Transactions on Services Computing*, 7(2):198–209, 2014.
8. Sarfraz Alam, Mohammad MR Chowdhury, and Josef Noll. Senaas: An event-driven sensor virtualization approach for internet of things cloud. In *2010 IEEE International Conference on Networked Embedded Systems for Enterprise Applications (NESEA)*, pages 1–6. IEEE, 2010.
9. Atif Alamri, Wasai Shadab Ansari, Mohammad Mehedi Hassan, M Shamim Hossain, Abdulhameed Alelaiwi, and M Anwar Hossain. A survey on sensor-cloud: architecture, applications, and approaches. *International Journal of Distributed Sensor Networks*, 9(2):917–923, 2013.
10. Florian Alt, Alireza Sahami Shirazi, Albrecht Schmidt, Urs Kramer, and Zahid Nawaz. Location-based crowdsourcing: extending crowdsourcing to the real world. In *Proceedings of the 6th Nordic Conference on Human-Computer Interaction: Extending Boundaries*, pages 13–22. ACM, 2010.
11. İ Kuban Altınel, Necati Aras, Evren Güney, and Cem Ersoy. Binary integer programming formulation and heuristics for differentiated coverage in heterogeneous sensor networks. *Computer Networks*, 52(12):2419–2431, 2008.
12. Maria J Antikainen and Heli K Vaataja. Rewarding in open innovation communities–how to motivate members. *International Journal of Entrepreneurship and Innovation Management*, 11(4):440–456, 2010.

© Springer International Publishing AG, part of Springer Nature 2018
A. Ghari Neiat, A. Bouguettaya, *Crowdsourcing of Sensor Cloud Services*,
https://doi.org/10.1007/978-3-319-91536-4

13. Michael Armbrust, Armando Fox, Rean Griffith, Anthony D Joseph, Randy Katz, Andy Konwinski, Gunho Lee, David Patterson, Ariel Rabkin, Ion Stoica, et al. A view of cloud computing. *Communications of the ACM*, 53(4):50–58, 2010.

14. Ashwinkumar Badanidiyuru, Robert Kleinberg, and Yaron Singer. Learning on a budget: posted price mechanisms for online procurement. In *Proceedings of the 13th ACM Conference on Electronic Commerce*, pages 128–145. ACM, 2012.

15. Eran Ben-Elia and Dick Ettema. Carrots versus sticks: Rewarding commuters for avoiding the rush-hour-a study of willingness to participate. *Journal of Transport policy*, 16(2):68–76, 2009.

16. Eran Ben-Elia and Dick Ettema. Rewarding rush-hour avoidance: A study of commuters' travel behavior. *Journal of Transportation Research Part A: Policy and Practice*, 45(7):567–582, 2011.

17. John Bethencourt, Amit Sahai, and Brent Waters. Ciphertext-policy attribute-based encryption. In *IEEE Symposium on Security and Privacy*, pages 321–334. IEEE, 2007.

18. Michiel CJ Bliemer, Matthijs Dicke-Ogenia, and Dick Ettema. Rewarding for avoiding the peak period: a synthesis of four studies in the netherlands. 2010.

19. Sunanda Bose and Nandini Mukherjee. Sensiaas: A sensor-cloud infrastructure with sensor virtualization. In *3rd International Conference on Cyber Security and Cloud Computing (CSCloud)*, pages 232–239. IEEE, 2016.

20. Denis Bouyssou, Didier Dubois, Henri Prade, and Marc Pirlot. *Decision Making Process: Concepts and Methods*. John Wiley & Sons, 2013.

21. George EP Box, Gwilym M Jenkins, Gregory C Reinsel, and Greta M Ljung. *Time series analysis: forecasting and control*. John Wiley & Sons, 2015.

22. Muhammed Fatih Bulut, Yavuz Selim Yilmaz, and Murat Demirbas. Crowdsourcing location-based queries. In *2011 IEEE International Conference on Pervasive Computing and Communications Workshops (PERCOM Workshops)*, pages 513–518. IEEE, 2011.

23. Jeffrey A Burke, Deborah Estrin, Mark Hansen, Andrew Parker, Nithya Ramanathan, Sasank Reddy, and Mani B Srivastava. Participatory sensing. *Center for Embedded Network Sensing*, 2006.

24. Gerardo Canfora, Massimiliano Di Penta, Raffaele Esposito, and Maria Luisa Villani. An approach for QoS-aware service composition based on genetic algorithms. In *Proceedings of the 7th annual conference on Genetic and evolutionary computation*, pages 1069–1075. ACM, 2005.

25. Gerardo Canfora, Massimiliano Di Penta, Raffaele Esposito, and Maria Luisa Villani. A framework for qos-aware binding and re-binding of composite web services. *Journal of Systems and Software*, 81(10):1754–1769, 2008.

26. Subarna Chatterjee and Sudip Misra. Target tracking using sensor-cloud: Sensor-target mapping in presence of overlapping coverage. *IEEE Communications Letters*, 18(8):1435–1438, 2014.

27. Ji-Dong Chen and Xiao-Feng Meng. Indexing future trajectories of moving objects in a constrained network. *Journal of Computer Science and Technology*, 22(2):245–251, 2007.

28. Nanxi Chen, Nicolás Cardozo, and Siobhán Clarke. Goal-driven service composition in mobile and pervasive computing. *IEEE Transactions on Services Computing*, 99, 2016.

29. Yohan Chon, Nicholas D Lane, Fan Li, Hojung Cha, and Feng Zhao. Automatically characterizing places with opportunistic crowdsensing using smartphones. In *Proceedings of the 2012 ACM Conference on Ubiquitous Computing*, pages 481–490. ACM, 2012.

30. Richard Chow, Philippe Golle, Markus Jakobsson, Elaine Shi, Jessica Staddon, Ryusuke Masuoka, and Jesus Molina. Controlling data in the cloud: outsourcing computation without outsourcing control. In *Proceedings of the 2009 ACM workshop on Cloud computing security*, pages 85–90. ACM, 2009.

31. Soon Ae Chun, Vijayalakshmi Atluri, and Nabil R. Adam. Using semantics for policy-based web service composition. *Journal of Distributed and Parallel Databases*, 18(1):37–64, 2005.

32. Wen-Yaw Chung, Pei-Shan Yu, and Chao-Jen Huang. Cloud computing system based on wireless sensor network. In *2013 Federated Conference on Computer Science and Information Systems (FedCSIS)*, pages 877–880. IEEE, 2013.

33. Peter Cohen, Robert Hahn, Jonathan Hall, Steven Levitt, and Robert Metcalfe. Using big data to estimate consumer surplus: The case of Uber. Technical report, National Bureau of Economic Research, 2016.

34. Justin Cranshaw, Eran Toch, Jason Hong, Aniket Kittur, and Norman Sadeh. Bridging the gap between physical location and online social networks. In *Proceedings of the 12th ACM international conference on Ubiquitous computing*, pages 119–128. ACM, 2010.

35. Sanjit Kumar Dash, Subasish Mohapatra, and Prasant Kumar Pattnaik. A survey on application of wireless sensor network using cloud computing. *International Journal of Computer science & Engineering Technologies (E-ISSN: 2044-6004)*, 1(4):50–55, 2010.

36. Edward Deci and Richard M Ryan. *Intrinsic Motivation and Self-Determination in Human Behavior*. Springer Science & Business Media, 1985.

37. Dingxiong Deng, Cyrus Shahabi, and Linhong Zhu. Task matching and scheduling for multiple workers in spatial crowdsourcing. In *Proceedings of the 23rd ACM SIGSPATIAL International Conference on Advances in Geographic Information Systems*, page 21. ACM, 2015.

38. Shuiguang Deng, Longtao Huang, Daning Hu, J Leon Zhao, and Zhaohui Wu. Mobility-enabled service selection for composite services. *IEEE Transactions on Services Computing*, 9(3):394–407, 2016.

39. Shuiguang Deng, Longtao Huang, Ying Li, and Jianwei Yin. Deploying data-intensive service composition with a negative selection algorithm. *International Journal of Web Services Research (IJWSR)*, 11(1):76–93, 2014.

40. Shuiguang Deng, Longtao Huang, Ying Li, Honggeng Zhou, Zhaohui Wu, Xiongfei Cao, Mikhail Yu Kataev, and Ling Li. Toward risk reduction for mobile service composition. *IEEE Transactions on Cybernetics*, 46(8):1807–1816, 2016.

41. Shuiguang Deng, Longtao Huang, Javid Taheri, Jianwei Yin, MengChu Zhou, and Albert Y Zomaya. Mobility-aware service composition in mobile communities. *IEEE Transactions on Systems, Man, and Cybernetics: Systems*, 47(3):555–568, 2017.

42. Shuiguang Deng, Longtao Huang, Hongyue Wu, and Zhaohui Wu. Constraints-driven service composition in mobile cloud computing. In *2016 IEEE International Conference on Web Services (ICWS)*, pages 228–235. IEEE, 2016.

43. Salvatore Distefano, Giovanni Merlino, and Antonio Puliafito. Sensing and actuation as a service: a new development for clouds. In *11th IEEE International Symposium on Network Computing and Applications (NCA)*, pages 272–275. IEEE, 2012.

44. Hongwei Dong, Liang Ma, and Joseph Broach. Promoting sustainable travel modes for commute tours: A comparison of the effects of home and work locations and employer-provided incentives. *International Journal of Sustainable Transportation*, 10(6):485–494, 2016.

45. Markus Eisenhauer, Peter Rosengren, and Pablo Antolin. Hydra: A development platform for integrating wireless devices and sensors into ambient intelligence systems. In *The Internet of Things*, pages 367–373. Springer, 2010.

46. Iria Estevez-Ayres, Pablo Basanta-Val, Marisol García-Valls, Jesús A Fisteus, and Luís Almeida. QoS-aware real-time composition algorithms for service-based applications. *IEEE Transactions on Industrial Informatics*, 5(3):278–288, 2009.

47. Patrick Th Eugster, Pascal A Felber, Rachid Guerraoui, and Anne-Marie Kermarrec. The many faces of publish/subscribe. *ACM Journal of Computing Surveys (CSUR)*, 35(2):114–131, 2003.

48. Hossein Falaki, Ratul Mahajan, Srikanth Kandula, Dimitrios Lymberopoulos, Ramesh Govindan, and Deborah Estrin. Diversity in smartphone usage. In *Proceedings of the 8th international conference on Mobile systems, applications, and services*, pages 179–194. ACM, 2010.

49. Brian Ferris, Kari Watkins, and Alan Borning. Onebusaway: results from providing real-time arrival information for public transit. In *Proceedings of the Conference on Human Factors in Computing Systems (SIGCHI)*, pages 1807–1816. ACM, 2010.

50. Giancarlo Fortino, Mukaddim Pathan, and Giuseppe Di Fatta. Bodycloud: Integration of cloud computing and body sensor networks. In *4th International Conference on Cloud Computing Technology and Science (CloudCom)*, pages 851–856. IEEE, 2012.

51. Ian Foster, Yong Zhao, Ioan Raicu, and Shiyong Lu. Cloud computing and grid computing 360-degree compared. In *Grid Computing Environments Workshop (GCE'08)*, pages 1–10. IEEE, 2008.

52. Ali Frihida, Danielle J Marceau, and Marius Theriault. Spatio-temporal object-oriented data model for disaggregate travel behavior. *Transactions in GIS*, 6(3):277–294, 2002.

53. Drew Fudenberg and Jean Tirole. Game theory, 1991. *Cambridge, Massachusetts*, 393:12, 1991.

54. Amir Hossein Gandomi and Amir Hossein Alavi. Krill herd: a new bio-inspired optimization algorithm. *In Journal of Communications in Nonlinear Science and Numerical Simulation*, 17(12):4831–4845, 2012.

55. Betsy George and Shashi Shekhar. Time-aggregated graphs for modeling spatio-temporal networks. In *Journal on Data Semantics XI*, pages 191–212. Springer, 2008.

56. Nawal Guermouche and Claude Godart. Composition of web services based on timed mediation. *International Journal of Next-Generation Computing (IJNGC)*, 5(1):26p, 2014.

57. Ikbel Guidara, Nawal Guermouche, Tarak Chaari, Said Tazi, and Mohamed Jmaiel. Pruning based service selection approach under QoS and temporal constraints. In *2014 IEEE International Conference on Web Services (ICWS)*, pages 9–16. IEEE, 2014.

58. Peter E Hart, Nils J Nilsson, and Bertram Raphael. A formal basis for the heuristic determination of minimum cost paths. *IEEE Transactions on Systems Science and Cybernetics*, 4(2):100–107, 1968.

59. Mohammad Mehedi Hassan, Biao Song, and Eui-Nam Huh. A framework of sensor-cloud integration opportunities and challenges. In *Proceedings of the 3rd International Conference on Ubiquitous Information Management and Communication*, pages 618–626. ACM, 2009.

60. Shibo He, Dong-Hoon Shin, Junshan Zhang, and Jiming Chen. Toward optimal allocation of location dependent tasks in crowdsensing. In *2014 IEEE International Conference on Computer Communications INFOCOM*, pages 745–753. IEEE, 2014.

61. Wendi Rabiner Heinzelman, Joanna Kulik, and Hari Balakrishnan. Adaptive protocols for information dissemination in wireless sensor networks. In *Proceedings of the 5th Annual ACM/IEEE International Conference on Mobile Computing and Networking*, pages 174–185. ACM, 1999.

62. Chien-Ju Ho, Shahin Jabbari, and Jennifer W Vaughan. Adaptive task assignment for crowdsourced classification. In *Proceedings of the 30th International Conference on Machine Learning (ICML-13)*, pages 534–542, 2013.

63. Chien-Ju Ho and Jennifer Wortman Vaughan. Online task assignment in crowdsourcing markets. In *AAAI*, volume 12, pages 45–51, 2012.

64. Jeff Howe. The rise of crowdsourcing. *Wired magazine*, 14(6):1–4, 2006.

65. Michael N Huhns and Munindar P Singh. Service-oriented computing: Key concepts and principles. *Journal IEEE Internet computing*, 9(1):75–81, 2005.

66. San-Yih Hwang, Ee-Peng Lim, Chien-Hsiang Lee, and Cheng-Hung Chen. Dynamic web service selection for reliable web service composition. *IEEE Transactions on Services Computing*, 1(2):104–116, 2008.

67. John Ibbotson, Christopher Gibson, Joel Wright, Peter Waggett, Petros Zerfos, Boleslaw Szymanski, and David J Thornley. Sensors as a service oriented architecture: Middleware for sensor networks. In *2010 Sixth International Conference on Intelligent Environments (IE),*, pages 209–214. IEEE, 2010.

68. George Iosifidis, Lin Gao, Jianwei Huang, and Leandros Tassiulas. Enabling crowdsourced mobile internet access. In *2014 IEEE International Conference on Computer Communications INFOCOM*, pages 451–459. IEEE, 2014.

69. Luis G Jaimes, Idalides Vergara-Laurens, and Alireza Chakeri. Spread, a crowd sensing incentive mechanism to acquire better representative samples. In *2014 IEEE International Conference on Pervasive Computing and Communications Workshops (PERCOM Workshops)*, pages 92–97. IEEE, 2014.

70. Luis G Jaimes, Idalides Vergara-Laurens, and Miguel A Labrador. A location-based incentive mechanism for participatory sensing systems with budget constraints. In *2012 IEEE International Conference on Pervasive Computing and Communications (PerCom)*, pages 103–108. IEEE, 2012.

71. Luis G Jaimes, Idalides J Vergara-Laurens, and Andrew Raij. A survey of incentive techniques for mobile crowd sensing. *IEEE Internet of Things Journal*, 2(5):370–380, 2015.

72. Hoyoung Jeung, Man Lung Yiu, Xiaofang Zhou, Christian S Jensen, and Heng Tao Shen. Discovery of convoys in trajectory databases. *Proceedings of the VLDB Endowment*, 1(1):1068–1080, 2008.

73. Wei Jiang, Tian Wu, Song-Lin Hu, and Zhi-Yong Liu. QoS-aware automatic service composition: A graph view. *Journal of Computer Science and Technology*, 26(5):837–853, 2011.

74. Hai Jin, Shadi Ibrahim, Tim Bell, Wei Gao, Dachuan Huang, and Song Wu. Cloud types and services. *Handbook of Cloud Computing*, pages 335–355, 2010.

75. David B Johnson and David A Maltz. Dynamic source routing in ad hoc wireless networks. In *Mobile computing*, pages 153–181. Springer, 1996.

76. Bonggi Jun, Bonghee Hong, and Byunggu Yu. Dynamic splitting policies of the adaptive 3dr-tree for indexing continuously moving objects. In *Database and expert systems applications*, pages 308–317. Springer, 2003.

77. Youn Chul Jung, Hee Yong Youn, and Eun Seok Lee. Boundary-based time partitioning with flattened r-tree for indexing ubiquitous objects. In *Mobile Ad-hoc and Sensor Networks*, pages 804–814. Springer, 2005.

78. Sanem Kabadayi, Adam Pridgen, and Christine Julien. Virtual sensors: Abstracting data from physical sensors. In *Proceedings of the 2006 International Symposium on World of Wireless, Mobile and Multimedia Networks*, pages 587–592. IEEE Computer Society, 2006.

79. Burak Kantarci and Hussein T Mouftah. Sensing services in cloud-centric internet of things: A survey, taxonomy and challenges. In *2015 IEEE International Conference on Communication Workshop (ICCW)*, pages 1865–1870. IEEE, 2015.

80. Leyla Kazemi and Cyrus Shahabi. Geocrowd: enabling query answering with spatial crowdsourcing. In *Proceedings of the 20th International Conference on Advances in Geographic Information Systems*, pages 189–198. ACM, 2012.

81. Samir Khuller, Anna Moss, and Joseph Seffi Naor. The budgeted maximum coverage problem. *Information Processing Letters*, 70(1):39–45, 1999.

82. Benjamin Klöpper, Fuyuki Ishikawa, and Shinichi Honiden. Service composition with pareto-optimality of time-dependent QoS attributes. In *International conference on Service-oriented Computing*, pages 635–640. Springer, 2010.

83. Sven Koenig and Maxim Likhachev. D* lite. In *AAAI/IAAI*, pages 476–483, 2002.

84. Sven Koenig and Maxim Likhachev. Improved fast replanning for robot navigation in unknown terrain. In *IEEE International Conference on Robotics and Automation, 2002 (ICRA'02)*, volume 1, pages 968–975. IEEE, 2002.

85. Sven Koenig and Maxim Likhachev. Real-time adaptive a*. In *Proceedings of the fifth international joint conference on Autonomous agents and multiagent systems*, pages 281–288. ACM, 2006.

86. Sven Koenig, Maxim Likhachev, and David Furcy. Lifelong planning a-star. *Artificial Intelligence*, 155(1):93–146, 2004.

87. Richard E Korf. Real-time heuristic search. *Artificial intelligence*, 42(2):189–211, 1990.

88. Iordanis Koutsopoulos. Optimal incentive-driven design of participatory sensing systems. In *2013 IEEE International Conference on Computer Communications INFOCOM*, pages 1402–1410. IEEE, 2013.

89. Vijay Krishna. *Auction theory*. Academic press, 2009.

90. Ioannis Krontiris and Andreas Albers. Monetary incentives in participatory sensing using multi-attributive auctions. *International Journal of Parallel, Emergent and Distributed Systems*, 27(4):317–336, 2012.

91. LP Dinesh Kumar, S Shakena Grace, Akshaya Krishnan, VM Manikandan, R Chinraj, and MR Sumalatha. Data filtering in wireless sensor networks using neural networks for storage in cloud. In *2012 International Conference on Recent Trends In Information Technology (ICRTIT)*, pages 202–205. IEEE, 2012.

92. Juong-Sik Lee and Baik Hoh. Dynamic pricing incentive for participatory sensing. *Pervasive and Mobile Computing*, 6(6):693–708, 2010.

93. Juong-Sik Lee and Baik Hoh. Sell your experiences: a market mechanism based incentive for participatory sensing. In *2010 IEEE International Conference on Pervasive Computing and Communications (PerCom)*, pages 60–68. IEEE, 2010.

94. Kevin Lee and Danny Hughes. System architecture directions for tangible cloud computing. In *2010 First ACIS International Symposium on Cryptography and Network Security, Data Mining and Knowledge Discovery, E-Commerce & Its Applications and Embedded Systems (CDEE)*, pages 258–262. IEEE, 2010.

95. Kevin Lee, David Murray, Danny Hughes, and Wouter Joosen. Extending sensor networks into the cloud using amazon web services. In *2010 IEEE International Conference on Networked Embedded Systems for Enterprise Applications (NESEA)*, pages 1–7. IEEE, 2010.

96. Ying Li, Xiaorong Zhang, Yu Yu Yin, and Yuanlei Lu. Towards functional dynamic reconfiguration for service-based applications. In *2011 IEEE World Congress on Services (SERVICES)*, pages 467–473. IEEE, 2011.

97. Maxim Likhachev, David I Ferguson, Geoffrey J Gordon, Anthony Stentz, and Sebastian Thrun. Anytime dynamic a*: An anytime, replanning algorithm. In *ICAPS*, pages 262–271, 2005.

98. Kwei-Jay Lin, Jing Zhang, Yanlong Zhai, and Bin Xu. The design and implementation of service process reconfiguration with end-to-end QoS constraints in SOA. *Service Oriented Computing and Applications*, 4(3):157–168, 2010.

99. Ruoshui Liu and Ian J Wassell. Opportunities and challenges of wireless sensor networks using cloud services. In *Proceedings of the workshop on Internet of Things and Service Platforms*, page 4. ACM, 2011.

100. Ahmed Lounis, Abdelkrim Hadjidj, Abdelmadjid Bouabdallah, and Yacine Challal. Secure and scalable cloud-based architecture for e-health wireless sensor networks. In *21st International Conference on Computer Communications and Networks (ICCCN)*, pages 1–7. IEEE, 2012.

101. Nebil Ben Mabrouk, Sandrine Beauche, Elena Kuznetsova, Nikolaos Georgantas, and Valérie Issarny. QoS-aware service composition in dynamic service oriented environments. In *Middleware 2009*, pages 123–142. Springer, 2009.

102. Sanjay Madria, Vimal Kumar, and Rashmi Dalvi. Sensor cloud: A cloud of virtual sensors. *Journal of IEEE Software*, 31(2):70–77, 2014.

103. Khaled Mahbub and Andrea Zisman. Replacement policies for service-based systems. In *2009 Workshops of Service-Oriented Computing (ICSOC/ServiceWave)*, pages 345–357. Springer, 2010.

104. Yannis Manolopoulos, Alexandros Nanopoulos, Apostolos N Papadopoulos, and Yannis Theodoridis. *R-Trees: Theory and Applications*. Springer Science & Business Media, 2010.

105. Afra J Mashhadi and Licia Capra. Quality control for real-time ubiquitous crowdsourcing. In *Proceedings of the 2nd international workshop on Ubiquitous crowdsouring*, pages 5–8. ACM, 2011.

106. Brahim Medjahed, Athman Bouguettaya, and Ahmed K Elmagarmid. Composing web services on the semantic web. *The International Journal on Very Large Data Bases (VLDB)*, 12(4):333–351, 2003.

107. Peter Mell and Timothy Grance. The NIST definition of cloud computing. *NIST special publication*, 800:145, 2011.

108. Diego Mendez and Miguel A Labrador. Density maps: Determining where to sample in participatory sensing systems. In *2012 Third FTRA International Conference on Mobile, Ubiquitous, and Intelligent Computing (MUSIC)*, pages 35–40. IEEE, 2012.

109. Sudip Misra, Subarna Chatterjee, and Mohammad S Obaidat. On theoretical modeling of sensor cloud: A paradigm shift from wireless sensor network. *IEEE Systems Journal*, pages 1–10, 2014.

110. Sudip Misra, Anuj Singh, Subarna Chatterjee, and Amit Kumar Mandal. QoS-aware sensor allocation for target tracking in sensor-cloud. *Ad Hoc Networks*, 33:140–153, 2015.

111. Mohamed F. Mokbel, Thanaa M. Ghanem, and Walid G. Aref. Spatio-temporal access methods. *IEEE Data Eng. Bull.*, 26(2):40–49, 2003.

112. Matteo Mordacchini, Andrea Passarella, Marco Conti, Stuart M Allen, Martin J Chorley, Gualtiero B Colombo, Vlad Tanasescu, and Roger M Whitaker. Crowdsourcing through cognitive opportunistic networks. *ACM Transactions on Autonomous and Adaptive Systems (TAAS)*, 10(2):13, 2015.

113. Arber Murturi, Burak Kantarci, and Sema F Oktug. A reference model for crowdsourcing as a service. In *2015 IEEE 4th International Conference on Cloud Networking (CloudNet)*, pages 64–66. IEEE, 2015.

114. Roger B Myerson. Optimal auction design. *Mathematics of operations research*, 6(1):58–73, 1981.

115. Mario A Nascimento and Jefferson RO Silva. Towards historical r-tree s. In *Proceedings of the 1998 ACM symposium on Applied Computing*, pages 235–240. ACM, 1998.

116. Nguyen Cao Hong Ngoc, Donghui Lin, Takao Nakaguchi, and Toru Ishida. QoS-aware service composition in mobile environments. In *7th International Conference on Service-Oriented Computing and Applications (SOCA)*, pages 97–104. IEEE, 2014.

117. Seog-Chan Oh, Ju-Yeon Lee, Seon-Hwa Cheong, Soo-Min Lim, Min-Woo Kim, Sang-Seok Lee, Jin-Bum Park, Sang-Do Noh, and Mye M Sohn. Wspr*: Web-service planner augmented with a* algorithm. In *IEEE Conference on Commerce and Enterprise Computing (CEC'09)*, pages 515–518. IEEE, 2009.

118. Michael Papazoglou. *Web services: principles and technology*. Addison-Wesley, 2008.

119. Mike P Papazoglou. Service-oriented computing: Concepts, characteristics and directions. In *Proceedings of the Fourth International Conference on Web Information Systems Engineering (WISE 2003)*, pages 3–12. IEEE, 2003.

120. Xin Peng, Jingxiao Gu, Tian Huat Tan, Jun Sun, Yijun Yu, Bashar Nuseibeh, and Wenyun Zhao. Crowdservice: Serving the individuals through mobile crowdsourcing and service composition. In *2016 31st IEEE/ACM International Conference on Automated Software Engineering (ASE)*, pages 214–219. IEEE, 2016.

121. Charith Perera, Arkady Zaslavsky, Peter Christen, and Dimitrios Georgakopoulos. Sensing as a service model for smart cities supported by internet of things. *Transactions on Emerging Telecommunications Technologies*, 25(1):81–93, 2014.

122. Michal Piorkowski, Natasa Sarafijanovic-Djukic, and Matthias Grossglauser. CRAWDAD dataset epfl/mobility (v. 2009-02-24). Downloaded from http://crawdad.org/epfl/mobility/20090224, February 2009.

123. V Rajesh, JM Gnanasekar, RS Ponmagal, and P Anbalagan. Integration of wireless sensor network with cloud. In *2010 International Conference on Recent Trends in Information, Telecommunication and Computing (ITC)*, pages 321–323. IEEE, 2010.

124. Sasank Reddy, Deborah Estrin, and Mani Srivastava. Recruitment framework for participatory sensing data collections. In *International Conference on Pervasive Computing*, pages 138–155. Springer, 2010.

125. Luis Henrique Oliveira Rios and Luiz Chaimowicz. A survey and classification of a* based best-first heuristic search algorithms. In *Advances in Artificial Intelligence–SBIA 2010*, pages 253–262. Springer, 2011.

126. Anne C Rouse. A preliminary taxonomy of crowdsourcing. *Proceedings of 21st Australasian Conference on Information Systems (ACIS)*, 76:1–10, 2010.

127. Hadi Saboohi, Amineh Amini, and Hassan Abolhassani. Failure recovery of composite semantic web services using subgraph replacement. In *International Conference on Computer and Communication Engineering ICCCE 2008*, pages 489–493. IEEE, 2008.

128. Umair Sadiq, Mohan Kumar, Andrea Passarella, and Marco Conti. Service composition in opportunistic networks: A load and mobility aware solution. *IEEE Transactions on Computers*, 64(8):2308–2322, 2015.

129. Simonas Šaltenis, Christian S Jensen, Scott T Leutenegger, and Mario A Lopez. *Indexing the positions of continuously moving objects*, volume 29. ACM, 2000.

130. Claude Elwood Shannon. A mathematical theory of communication. *ACM SIGMOBILE Mobile Computing and Communications Review*, 5(1):3–55, 2001.

131. Xiang Sheng, Jian Tang, Xuejie Xiao, and Guoliang Xue. Sensing as a service: Challenges, solutions and future directions. *IEEE Sensors Journal*, 13(10):3733–3741, 2013.

132. Xiang Sheng, Xuejie Xiao, Jian Tang, and Guoliang Xue. Sensing as a service: A cloud computing system for mobile phone sensing. In *Sensors 2012*, pages 1–4. IEEE, 2012.

133. Dongyoun Shin, Stefan Müller Arisona, Sofia Georgakopoulou, Gerhard Schmitt, and Sungah Kim. A crowdsourcing urban simulation platform on smartphone technology: Strategies for urban data visualization and transportation mode detection. In *Proceedings of the 30th eCAADe Conference*, pages 377–384, 2012.

134. Yaron Singer and Manas Mittal. Pricing mechanisms for crowdsourcing markets. In *Proceedings of the 22nd international conference on World Wide Web*, pages 1157–1166, 2013.

135. Adish Singla and Andreas Krause. Truthful incentives in crowdsourcing tasks using regret minimization mechanisms. In *Proceedings of the 22nd international conference on World Wide Web*, pages 1167–1178, 2013.

136. Katarina Stanoevska-Slabeva and Thomas Wozniak. Cloud basics–an introduction to cloud computing. *Journal of Grid and Cloud Computing*, pages 47–61, 2010.

137. Aaron Steinfeld, John Zimmerman, Anthony Tomasic, Daisy Yoo, and Rafae Aziz. Mobile transit information from universal design and crowdsourcing. *Transportation Research Record: Journal of the Transportation Research Board*, (2217):95–102, 2011.

138. Anthony Stentz. Optimal and efficient path planning for partially-known environments. In *Proceedings of 1994 IEEE International Conference on Robotics and Automation*, pages 3310–3317. IEEE, 1994.

139. Wen Sun and Chen-Khong Tham. A spatio-temporal incentive scheme with consumer demand awareness for participatory sensing. In *2015 IEEE International Conference on Communications (ICC)*, pages 6363–6369. IEEE, 2015.

140. Lu-An Tang, Yu Zheng, Jing Yuan, Jiawei Han, Alice Leung, Chih-Chieh Hung, and Wen-Chih Peng. On discovery of traveling companions from streaming trajectories. In *2012 IEEE 28th International Conference Data Engineering (ICDE) on*, pages 186–197. IEEE, 2012.

141. Maolin Tang and Lifeng Ai. A hybrid genetic algorithm for the optimal constrained web service selection problem in web service composition. In *2010 IEEE Congress on Evolutionary Computation (CEC)*, pages 1–8. IEEE, 2010.

142. Yufei Tao and Dimitris Papadias. The mv3r-tree: A spatio-temporal access method for timestamp and interval queries. In *Proceedings of Very Large Data Bases Conference (VLDB), 11–14 September, Rome*, 2001.

143. Y Theodoridis, Michael Vazirgiannis, and Timos Sellis. Spatio-temporal indexing for large multimedia applications. In *Proceedings of the Third IEEE International Conference on Multimedia Computing and Systems*, pages 441–448. IEEE, 1996.

144. Niwat Thepvilojanapong, Kai Zhang, Tomoya Tsujimori, Yoshikatsu Ohta, Yunlong Zhao, and Yoshito Tobe. Participation-aware incentive for active crowd sensing. In *2013 IEEE 10th International Conference on High Performance Computing and Communications & 2013 IEEE International Conference on Embedded and Ubiquitous Computing (HPCC_EUC)*, pages 2127–2134. IEEE, 2013.

145. Hien To, Cyrus Shahabi, and Leyla Kazemi. A server-assigned spatial crowdsourcing framework. *ACM Transactions on Spatial Algorithms and Systems*, 1(1):2, 2015.

146. Calvin P Tribby and Paul A Zandbergen. High-resolution spatio-temporal modeling of public transit accessibility. *Journal of Applied Geography*, 34:345–355, 2012.

147. Wei-Tek Tsai, Xin Sun, and Janaka Balasooriya. Service-oriented cloud computing architecture. In *2010 Seventh International Conference on Information Technology: New Generations (ITNG)*, pages 684–689. IEEE, 2010.

148. Peter JM Van Laarhoven and Emile HL Aarts. Simulated annealing. In *Simulated Annealing: Theory and Applications*, pages 7–15. Springer, 1987.

149. Marcos R Vieira, Petko Bakalov, and Vassilis J Tsotras. On-line discovery of flock patterns in spatio-temporal data. In *Proceedings of the 17th ACM SIGSPATIAL International Conference on Advances in Geographic Information Systems*, pages 286–295. ACM, 2009.

150. Florian Wagner, Adrian Klein, Benjamin Klöpper, Fuyuki Ishikawa, and Shinichi Honiden. Multi-objective service composition with time-and input-dependent QoS. In *2012 IEEE 19th International Conference on Web Services (ICWS)*, pages 234–241. IEEE, 2012.

151. Donggen Wang and Tao Cheng. A spatio-temporal data model for activity-based transport demand modelling. *International Journal of Geographical Information Science*, 15(6):561–585, 2001.

152. Hao Wang, Yunlong Zhao, Yang Li, Kai Zhang, Niwat Thepvilojanapong, and Yoshito Tobe. An optimized directional distribution strategy of the incentive mechanism in SenseUtil-based participatory sensing environment. In *2013 IEEE Ninth International Conference on Mobile Ad-hoc and Sensor Networks (MSN)*, pages 67–71. IEEE, 2013.

153. Jianping Wang. Exploiting mobility prediction for dependable service composition in wireless mobile ad hoc networks. *IEEE Transactions on Services Computing*, 4(1):44–55, 2011.

154. Wei Wang, Kevin Lee, and David Murray. Integrating sensors with the cloud using dynamic proxies. In *23rd International Symposium on Personal Indoor and Mobile Radio Communications (PIMRC)*, pages 1466–1471. IEEE, 2012.

155. Bin Wu, Shuiguang Deng, Ying Li, Jian Wu, and Jianwei Yin. AWSP: an automatic web service planner based on heuristic state space search. In *2011 IEEE International Conference on Web Services (ICWS)*, pages 403–410. IEEE, 2011.

156. Mingjun Xiao, Jie Wu, Liusheng Huang, Yunsheng Wang, and Cong Liu. Multi-task assignment for crowdsensing in mobile social networks. In *2015 IEEE Conference on Computer Communications INFOCOM*, pages 2227–2235. IEEE, 2015.

157. Dejun Yang, Guoliang Xue, Xi Fang, and Jian Tang. Crowdsourcing to smartphones: incentive mechanism design for mobile phone sensing. In *Proceedings of the 18th annual international conference on Mobile computing and networking*, pages 173–184. ACM, 2012.

158. Zhen Ye, Xiaofang Zhou, and Athman Bouguettaya. Genetic algorithm based QoS-aware service compositions in cloud computing. In *International Conference on Database Systems for Advanced Applications*, pages 321–334. Springer, Berlin, Heidelberg, 2011.

159. Jennifer Yick, Biswanath Mukherjee, and Dipak Ghosal. Wireless sensor network survey. *Journal of Computer Networks*, 52(12):2292–2330, 2008.

160. Qi Yu and Athman Bouguettaya. Framework for web service query algebra and optimization. *ACM Transactions on the Web (TWEB)*, 2(1):6, 2008.

161. Qi Yu, Xumin Liu, Athman Bouguettaya, and Brahim Medjahed. Deploying and managing web services: issues, solutions, and directions. *The International Journal on Very Large Data Bases (VLDB)*, 17(3):537–572, 2008.

162. Madoka Yuriyama and Takayuki Kushida. Sensor-cloud infrastructure-physical sensor management with virtualized sensors on cloud computing. In *2010 13th International Conference on Network-Based Information Systems (NBiS)*, pages 1–8. IEEE, 2010.

163. Madoka Yuriyama, Takayuki Kushida, and Mayumi Itakura. A new model of accelerating service innovation with sensor-cloud infrastructure. In *2011 Annual SRII Global Conference*, pages 308–314. IEEE, 2011.

164. Liangzhao Zeng, Boualem Benatallah, Anne H. H. Ngu, Marlon Dumas, Jayant Kalagnanam, and Henry Chang. QoS-aware middleware for web services composition. *IEEE Transactions on Software Engineering*, 30(5):311–327, 2004.

165. Yanlong Zhai, Jing Zhang, and Kwei-Jay Lin. SOA middleware support for service process reconfiguration with end-to-end QoS constraints. In *IEEE International Conference on Web Services (ICWS 2009)*, pages 815–822. IEEE, 2009.

166. Qi Zhang, Lu Cheng, and Raouf Boutaba. Cloud computing: state-of-the-art and research challenges. *Journal of Internet Services and Applications*, 1(1):7–18, 2010.

167. Tao Zhang, JianFeng Ma, Qi Li, Ning Xi, and Cong Sun. Trust-based service composition in multi-domain environments under time constraint. *Science China Information Sciences*, 57(9):1–16, 2014.

168. John Zimmerman, Anthony Tomasic, Charles Garrod, Daisy Yoo, Chaya Hiruncharoenvate, Rafae Aziz, Nikhil Ravi Thiruvengadam, Yun Huang, and Aaron Steinfeld. Field trial of tiramisu: crowd-sourcing bus arrival times to spur co-design. In *Proceedings of the SIGCHI Conference on Human Factors in Computing Systems*, pages 1677–1686. ACM, 2011.

Printed in the United States
By Bookmasters